Unmasking Your Authenticity

Navigating Late Diagnosis: Embracing Your
Autistic Self and Nurturing Your Inner Child

Hillary Sartor

Table of Contents

Introduction

I magine a life where you no longer need to hide who you are—where you can shed the layers of societal expectations and immerse yourself in the beauty of your authentic self. This book is an invitation to embark on that journey, a profound act of self-love and acceptance designed specifically for late-diagnosed autistic adults and individuals with ADHD. If you find yourself seeking guidance on unmasking and embracing your true identity while connecting with your inner child, you have come to the right place.

Living in a world that often misunderstands or overlooks neurodiversity, many of us have learned to navigate social environments by concealing our true selves. This process, commonly called masking, goes beyond mere social adaptation. It involves deeply ingrained behaviors touching various aspects of our daily lives. Masking shapes how we interact with others, perceive ourselves, and function in society. For many, it becomes second nature—a survival mechanism developed over years of trying to fit into a world not built with us in mind.

Yet, living behind these masks comes at a significant cost. Continuous masking can lead to emotional exhaustion, anxiety, and a sense of disconnect from one's true self. It's like wearing a costume day in and day out, never fully being able to take it off and be comfortable in one's skin. Understanding the complexities of masking is crucial to unraveling its impact on our mental health and overall well-being. The psychological implications run deep, and their roots are often entangled in both personal experiences and cultural narratives surrounding autism and ADHD.

The history of masking within the autistic and ADHD communities reveals a tapestry of resilience and ingenuity. Many individuals have had no choice but to conform to societal norms to survive while yearning for a space where they could be themselves. The journey of unmasking, therefore, is about more than discarding these adaptive behaviors. It's about reclaiming one's identity, embracing vulnerability, and finding strength in authenticity. It's about breaking free from the confines of imposed identities to discover the multifaceted, vibrant person beneath.

This book aims to weave a rich narrative celebrating diverse voices and experiences. Each person's journey of unmasking is unique, shaped by their personal histories, cultural contexts, and individual challenges. By incorporating a broad range of perspectives, we seek to honor the richness of neurodiversity and create an inclusive narrative that resonates with all readers. Whether you are beginning this journey yourself or supporting a loved one, understanding how people experience and cope with masking will foster empathy and connection.

Our exploration of unmasking is not just theoretical; it's practical. I believe in providing insights and actionable steps that empower you to start your unmasking journey effectively. Whether looking for ways to nurture your inner child or strategies to navigate your professional environment authentically, this book offers concrete advice tailored to your needs.

Connecting with your inner child is a critical component of the unmasking process. Many of us have lost touch with the pure, unfiltered joy and curiosity that characterized our early years, burying these qualities under layers of adult responsibilities and societal pressures. Reconnecting with this aspect of ourselves is therapeutic and essential for holistic self-acceptance. Through guided exercises and reflective practices, I encourage you to rediscover the playfulness and creativity within you—qualities that mask-free living seeks to bring back to the forefront.

Navigating professional settings poses challenges and opportunities, in addition to nurturing your inner child. The workplace's structured environments and expectations can feel particularly daunting. However, open communication, self-advocacy, and setting boundaries can pave the way for more genuine interactions and fulfilling professional experiences. This book provides strategies to help you balance authenticity with the practicalities of career advancement and workplace dynamics.

Throughout this book, we'll explore various facets of daily life that interact with your journey toward unmasking. Relationships, for instance, play a pivotal role in shaping our sense of self. Whether it's friendships, romantic partnerships, or family ties, these connections can reinforce our masks or support our efforts to unmask. Let's delve into ways to communicate your needs to loved ones, build supportive networks, and foster relationships that celebrate rather than conceal your true self.

Finally, self-care and mental health must be considered in this conversation. Unmasking is an ongoing process requiring patience, resilience, and continuous self-compassion. I discuss techniques for managing stress, recognizing burnout, and cultivating a lifestyle that prioritizes your well-being. Remember, unmasking is not a destination but a journey where every step towards authenticity is an accomplishment worth celebrating. Additionally, this is a journey that is best navigated with others. Please remember to seek the assistance of a loved one or therapist when needed, and remember that it's okay to ask for help.

By the end of this book, I hope you will feel equipped and inspired to undertake your own journey of unmasking. Embracing your true self is a radical act of courage, a statement that you are worthy of love and acceptance precisely as you are. I wish this book serves as both a guide and a companion as you navigate the path towards self-discovery and authenticity.

Welcome to your journey. Let's unmask together.

Understanding Masking: A Comprehensive Introduction

U nderstanding masking involves exploring how neurodivergent individuals conceal their true selves to fit societal norms. Masking often begins unconsciously, with people adjusting their behavior to avoid stigma and gain acceptance. Over time, these behaviors can become second nature, even if they lead to emotional and psychological strain. For late-diagnosed autistic adults and those with ADHD, acknowledging these behaviors is an essential step toward self-acceptance and mental well-being.

This chapter will explore the various dimensions of masking, from its definition to its psychological impacts. We will examine how conscious and unconscious methods affect everything from daily interactions to long-term identity formation. Through real-life examples and research findings, this chapter highlights the toll of sustained masking and underscores the need for more inclusive and accepting environments. The journey of unmasking, though challenging, holds the promise of relief and authenticity, helping individuals embrace their authentic selves while navigating a world that often feels unaccommodating.

Exploring the Definition and Psychological Implications of Masking

Masking, a concept well-known among neurodivergent individuals, refers to hiding or suppressing one's true self to fit societal expectations. This subpoint aims to explore the definition and the psychological implications of masking, setting the stage for understanding its profound effects on individuals with neurodivergent traits like autism and ADHD.

One way individuals mask is through conscious efforts to blend in. This might include mimicking social behaviors they observe in others, such as maintaining eye contact, adjusting their tone of voice, or using specific facial expressions. These actions are consciously controlled in an attempt to meet societal norms. On the other hand, there are unconscious methods of masking where individuals may not even realize they're doing it. For instance, an autistic person might suppress stimming (repetitive movements or sounds) without realizing why, simply because they've been conditioned over time to believe these behaviors are inappropriate.

The emotional and mental toll of sustained masking cannot be overstated. Constantly monitoring and modifying behavior to appear 'normal' can lead to chronic stress and fatigue. This effort to conform often leaves individuals mentally and physically drained. The strain of pretending to be someone else means they rarely have an opportunity to relax and be themselves, resulting in isolation and loneliness. Furthermore, the internal conflict between their true self and the persona they project can lead to a fractured sense of identity.

The link between masking and conditions such as anxiety, depression, and identity struggles is significant. The continuous pressure to conceal one's authentic self often exacerbates anxiety and can lead to depressive episodes. Many people feel deep grief and loss over their hidden identity, wondering who they might have been without feeling the need to hide or who they indeed are beneath the facade. This grief and identity struggle add layers to the already complex mental health challenges they face. The disconnect from their true self can hinder personal growth and self-acceptance, making it harder to form genuine relationships and community bonds.

Providing examples helps illustrate how masking manifests in everyday situations for late-diagnosed autistic adults and individuals with ADHD. For instance, at a workplace meeting, an autistic adult might take great care to monitor their body language and facial expression, ensuring they appear engaged and enthusiastic, even if they are overwhelmed by sensory input. Similarly, a person with ADHD might spend considerable effort keeping their impulsivity in check during conversations, which can be exhausting and make it difficult to participate fully. These day-to-day battles highlight the constant vigilance required to maintain the mask, often leading to burnout.

By exploring how individuals mask, consciously and unconsciously, we gain insight into the varied strategies employed to navigate a world that often feels unaccommodating. Understanding this helps us appreciate the tremendous effort involved and paves the way for creating more inclusive environments. Shifting away from a one-size-fits-all approach to social interaction can help reduce the burden of masking and promote greater acceptance of neurodiversity.

The detailed emotional and mental toll reveals the hidden costs of masking. Chronic stress, fatigue, and a fragmented sense of self can lead to severe mental health issues. Recognizing these impacts encourages supportive measures that address the unique needs of neurodivergent individuals. Providing safe environments where authentic freedom of expression can exist without fear of judgment or repercussion is crucial.

Finally, examining the link between masking and related conditions underscores the urgent need for mental health support tailored to neurodivergent experiences. Awareness and intervention can alleviate some psychological burdens associated with prolonged masking. Support groups, therapy focused on acceptance and commitment, and community-building activities can offer relief and foster a sense of belonging.

Providing Historical Context and Prevalence of Masking

To fully grasp the significance of masking within the autism and ADHD communities, we first need to trace its origins. Masking, often referred to as "camouflaging," has historical roots in the attempts by neurodivergent individuals to blend into neurotypical society. The term emerged from broader discussions on neurodiversity, which began gaining traction in the late 20th century. These conversations challenged traditional views on cognitive differences, advocating for a more inclusive understanding of varying neurological conditions. Historically, the neurodiversity movement provided a framework for recognizing behaviors like masking as not merely aberrant but as adaptive strategies developed in response to societal pressures.

Critical moments in recognizing and studying masking behaviors highlight its growing prominence within clinical and research settings. In the early 2000s, scholarly attention began focusing on the distinctive ways autistic individuals and those with ADHD adapted their behaviors in social contexts. Pioneering studies shed light on how these individuals consciously or unconsciously mimicked neurotypical behaviors to avoid stigma or rejection. For instance, research into gender differences revealed that girls and women often masked their symptoms more effectively, leading to delayed diagnoses compared to their male counterparts. This increased awareness spurred further investigations, resulting in significant breakthroughs in understanding the pervasiveness and complexity of masking.

Research and personal accounts are invaluable in showcasing the widespread occurrence of masking among late-diagnosed autistic adults and individuals with ADHD. Studies have demonstrated that many neurodivergent individuals resort to masking as a means of securing social acceptance at the cost of their mental well-being. Autistic adults and those with ADHD often share poignant stories of how masking led to a sense of disconnection from their true identities. These narratives illustrate the substantial prevalence of masking behaviors. Evidently, late diagnosis compounds these challenges, as individuals may spend years unaware of their neurodivergent status, all while striving to conform to societal expectations.

Without realizing it, I may have been displaying traits of autism myself. It was eye-opening to learn how autism can present differently in women and girls, often leading to missed or delayed diagnosis. Exploring this further has given me a deeper understanding of neurodiversity and a greater appreciation for the unique traits and perspectives that individuals on the autism spectrum bring to the world.

The evolving understanding of masking as a coping mechanism highlights its role in managing societal pressures. Historically, societal norms have favored conformity, compelling neurodivergent individuals to mask their unique traits. Modern perspectives, however, recognize masking as a double-edged sword. While it can facilitate smoother social interactions, prolonged masking exerts a heavy toll on mental health. Autistic individuals and those with ADHD who engage in sustained masking behaviors often report heightened anxiety, depression, and burnout. The physical symptoms of masking include headaches, gastrointestinal issues, muscle tension, sleep disturbances, and weakened immune systems. This reevaluation underscores the need for greater societal acceptance and support for neurodivergent individuals, enabling them to convey their true selves without the perception of judgment or ostracization.

Understanding the origins of masking within neurodiverse contexts is crucial for comprehending its impact on late-diagnosed individuals. Early discussions about neurodiversity were instrumental in framing behaviors like masking as protective responses rather than purely symptomatic actions. Revisiting these origins helps us appreciate masking's adaptive function, revealing its deep-seated roots in the human need for belonging and acceptance.

Highlighting fundamental studies and breakthroughs in recognizing masking behaviors offers valuable insights into its development. Notable research in the past decade has drawn connections between social camouflaging and diagnostic delays in autism and ADHD. Findings indicate that successful masking can obscure clinical symptoms, complicating accurate and timely diagnoses. By examining these pivotal moments in research, we understand how masking has evolved from an overlooked behavior to a focal point in understanding neurodivergence.

Research findings and personal testimonies bring to life the far-reaching impacts of masking on individuals diagnosed later in life. Quantitative studies reveal alarming statistics: a large percentage of late-diagnosed autistic adults and those with ADHD admit to constant masking in social situations. Meanwhile, qualitative accounts provide a human dimension, depicting the emotional exhaustion and identity struggles stemming from years of self-suppression. These sources comprehensively portray masking's prevalence and profound effects on neurodivergent lives.

Exploring masking as a reaction to societal norms and pressures emphasizes its multifaceted nature. Societal acceptance of diversity remains limited, prompting neurodivergent individuals to camouflage their behaviors to align with mainstream expectations. This ongoing adaptation process reflects a broader narrative about the intersection of individual identity and collective societal standards. Understanding this dynamic is essential for fostering environments where authenticity is valued over conformity, reducing the pressure on neurodivergent individuals to perpetually mask.

Highlighting Distinctions Between Masking and Social Adaptation

Masking and everyday social adaptation can often be confused, yet they are vastly different concepts. Masking involves concealing one's true self to gain social acceptance or avoid stigma. For example, an autistic adult might mimic typical facial expressions or suppress stimming behaviors to fit in. This is markedly distinct from the minor adjustments everyone makes to adhere to general social norms, such as dressing appropriately for a formal event. While both require changes in behavior, masking demands a more profound, more sustained suppression of one's natural instincts and preferences.

Everyday social adaptation tends to be situational and transient. For instance, people may modify their tone during a job interview but revert to their natural speaking style among friends. In contrast, masking behaviors are persistent and pervasive, affecting many aspects of daily life. Over time, these intentional efforts to hide one's neurodivergent traits can lead to a disconnect between one's external persona and internal identity, which is rarely the case with routine social adaptations.

Understanding this distinction is crucial for late-diagnosed autistic adults and individuals with ADHD. These groups often grapple with heightened societal expectations to conform, leading them to engage in masking behaviors beyond simple adaptation. Unlike neurotypical individuals, who may feel only mild discomfort when adjusting to social norms, neurodivergent individuals experience significant emotional and cognitive dissonance when masking, making their social interactions far more taxing (Miller et al., 2021).

Masking requires more than just adhering to social etiquette; it involves deeply suppressing one's true self. Autistic adults, for instance, might refrain from expressing their interests or engaging in behaviors that bring them comfort, such as fidgeting or focusing intently on a particular topic. This differs substantially from adapting to social norms, which might involve more superficial changes like using polite language or maintaining appropriate eye contact.

The suppression entailed in masking affects mental health and well-being. When individuals mask, they often hide their emotions, reactions, and even physical discomforts, creating a façade that can be exhausting to maintain. This repeated suppression means one does not just adapt to fit into specific situations but essentially lives behind a mask, which can result in feelings of isolation and a lack of authentic connections with others.

For late-diagnosed autistic adults and individuals with ADHD, this suppression becomes even more pronounced. Having spent years without a diagnosis, many have developed sophisticated masks to navigate a world not designed for their needs. The realization of their neurodivergence later in life often comes with the stark revelation of how much of themselves they have kept hidden. Unpacking these layers of suppression can be both liberating and daunting, requiring a delicate balance between embracing authenticity and managing societal expectations. Take note of the moments when situations or activities bring exhaustion. These times may indicate when you were masking and perhaps were unaware of it.

Additionally, there may be moments when your inner child becomes wide-eyed and excited about an activity or event. Times like these need extra attention. Embrace and savor the moments that make you feel truly alive, as they are worth treasuring and embracing.

Navigating social expectations poses additional complexities for late-diagnosed autistic adults and individuals with ADHD. Unlike those diagnosed earlier, who might receive support and accommodations growing up, late-diagnosed individuals often have to relearn how to interact with the world. They must reconcile the coping mechanisms they developed independently with their newfound understanding of their neurodivergence.

Another layer of complexity is the intersectionality of multiple neurodivergent traits. An individual with both autism and ADHD, for instance, might find it particularly challenging to maintain focus in social settings while also trying to adhere to socially accepted behaviors. The constant juggling act between controlling impulsivity, managing sensory overload, and presenting a "normal" front can be overwhelmingly exhausting.

These challenges are compounded by societal misconceptions and limited awareness about neurodivergent conditions. Many late-diagnosed individuals face skepticism or misunderstanding from peers, family, and even healthcare providers, further complicating their journey toward self-acceptance. Educating oneself and others about the unique experiences and needs of neurodivergent individuals becomes essential in navigating these social landscapes effectively.

Prolonged masking carries significant risks for mental health and identity formation. The continuous effort to hide one's true self can lead to escalating stress, depression, and anxiety. Individuals may feel like they are living a lie, causing a profound alienation from others and themselves. Over time, this can erode self-esteem and lead to burnout, where the person is unable to maintain the mask, resulting in complete emotional and physical collapse.

One of the most alarming risks associated with prolonged masking is its impact on identity development. Constantly pretending to be someone else can make it difficult for individuals to understand who they are. This identity confusion can extend into adulthood, making it challenging to form authentic relationships or pursue genuine interests and goals.

Using Case Studies to Provide Diverse Perspectives on Masking

One of the most profound ways to understand masking is through personal stories illustrating individuals' struggles and breakthroughs. I received my official diagnosis of ADHD and autism at the age of 46. All my life, I felt different but couldn't pinpoint why. I excelled in academics yet found social interactions draining. I mimicked others' behaviors to fit in, unknowingly masking my true self. This led to a sense of disconnection and chronic exhaustion as I constantly monitored my actions, striving for acceptance. My diagnosis left me feeling as though I didn't know who I really was under my mask.

My breakthrough came when I found other late-diagnosed autistic adults through social media. Their shared experiences offered a mirror into my life. I began to recognize my behaviors as masking and understood the toll they had taken on my mental health. Realizing these patterns allowed me to start unmasking gradually. Initially, this process was daunting; I feared rejection and judgment from those around me. I realized I was happiest when I let my inner child come out to play. I began to laugh more freely, dance like nobody was watching, and allow myself to dream boldly once again. Yet, embracing authenticity brought immense relief and clarity about my identity.

Unmasking also led to significant changes in my relationships. Friends who genuinely accepted me provided a supportive environment, whereas others grew more distant. My confidence grew as I became more authentic, fostering deeper connections with like-minded individuals. My journey exemplifies the masking challenges and the unmasking triumphs, highlighting the importance of self-awareness and community support.

Exploring the factors that lead individuals to realize their masking behaviors often reveals intricate layers of societal and personal influences. For me, several key moments catalyzed this realization. During my childhood, subtle encouragements from teachers and peers to conform masked my natural tendencies. Over time, these became ingrained survival mechanisms. My perfectionist tendencies further fueled the masking as I strove to meet perceived expectations.

In adulthood, my professional life demanded high social interaction, amplifying the stress from my masking behaviors.

Frequent burnout episodes served as red flags, indicating something deeper was wrong. However, it wasn't until a television show personality shared their autistic experience with masking that I began to consider the possibility for myself. This revelation set me on a path of introspection, leading me to seek out formal diagnosis and support.

The critical factor was finding a community where masking was openly discussed and understood. Through conversations with others who experienced similar struggles, I saw my own behaviors reflected back at me. This external validation was crucial in helping me identify and address my masking, marking the beginning of my unmasking journey.

Contrasting perspectives on masking can provide valuable insights into its multifaceted nature. Take John, a late-diagnosed individual with ADHD whose experience with masking differed significantly from my own. Unlike me, who masked primarily to fit in socially, John's masking focused on managing his impulsivity and inattentiveness. Growing up, he faced constant reprimands for being "too much" or "not focused," which led him to develop coping strategies to appear more neurotypical.

John's masking involved intense self-regulation, such as meticulously planning his day to avoid distractions and maintaining a calm demeanor in social settings. This required immense effort and often left him exhausted and disconnected from his true self. However, his unmasking journey began after a series of failed relationships and job losses, highlighting the unsustainable nature of his coping mechanisms. Seeking therapy, John discovered the concept of masking, which resonated deeply with his experiences.

Through therapeutic support, John learned to embrace his neurodivergence rather than suppress it. He started implementing practical strategies tailored to his needs, such as using tools and apps for task management and prioritizing environments that accommodated his sensory sensitivities. This shift from masking to self-acceptance improved his well-being and enhanced his relationships and professional life.

Unmasking has significant impacts on an individual's self-awareness and relationships. For myself, the process of unmasking brought a profound sense of liberation. I began to better understand my preferences, strengths, and limitations, enabling me to make choices that aligned with my true self. This newfound self-awareness translated into greater self-compassion and reduced the internal conflicts I previously experienced.

Similarly, John's unmasking journey led to a deeper understanding of his ADHD and its effects on his life. By acknowledging his neurodivergent traits, he could advocate for himself more effectively, personally and professionally. This self-advocacy fostered a sense of empowerment, allowing him to navigate life's challenges with more resilience and confidence.

In both cases, unmasking transformed our relationships. My authenticity attracted friends who valued my true self, creating more meaningful and supportive connections. For John, unmasking helped him communicate his needs more clearly, improving his relationships with family, friends, and colleagues. The process of unmasking, while challenging, ultimately enriched our lives by fostering genuine connections and a stronger sense of self.

Understanding masking helps people see how it affects someone's mind and daily life. This knowledge can give them the understanding and tools to support individuals who think differently.

We have explored the concept of masking and its psychological implications for late-diagnosed autistic adults and individuals with ADHD. Masking is a complex and often unconscious effort to hide one's true self to fit societal expectations. This behavior ranges from mimicking social cues to suppressing natural behaviors, all in a bid to appear "normal." The consequences of masking are profound, leading to chronic stress, fatigue, and a fractured sense of identity.

In our discussion, we looked into conscious and unconscious methods of masking. These behaviors often require significant mental and emotional energy, leaving individuals exhausted and disconnected. Over time, constant masking can exacerbate anxiety and depression and contribute to a deep sense of loss. Many neurodivergent individuals grapple with who they might have been if not for the pressure to conform, highlighting the significant impact on their mental health and personal development.

We also examined how societal norms compel neurodivergent individuals to mask. Historical and modern perspectives show that while masking can temporarily ease social interactions, it comes at the cost of one's well-being. The stories we've shared, including my own and John's experiences, shed light on the varied ways masking manifests and the journey toward unmasking. My journey revealed the importance of support and self-awareness, while John highlighted the necessity for tailored strategies that align with one's unique needs.

Another critical point was the distinction between everyday social adaptation and masking. Social adaptation tends to be situational and relatively superficial, such as adjusting tone during an interview. In contrast, masking involves a more profound suppression of one's natural instincts and preferences, affecting many aspects of life. This profound level of suppression is mentally taxing and contributes to feelings of isolation and identity confusion.

Considering the broader implications, it's clear that prolonged masking has significant consequences. The continuous need to hide one's true self can lead to significant mental health issues, including burnout and identity crises. For late-diagnosed individuals, the journey to unmasking can be particularly challenging, requiring a balance between embracing authenticity and managing societal expectations.

It's crucial to create environments where neurodivergent individuals feel safe to express themselves authentically. This includes educating society about the impacts of masking and fostering greater acceptance of neurodiversity. By valuing authenticity over conformity, we can reduce the pressure to mask and support better mental health outcomes.

As we conclude this chapter, let's reflect on how understanding masking can lead to more inclusive and supportive communities. What steps can we take to ensure everyone feels seen and accepted for who they are? The journey of unmasking is profoundly personal, but sharing these experiences helps build empathy and drive change in our society.

The Discovery: Unmasking After Late Diagnosis

U nmasking after receiving a late diagnosis of autism or ADHD can be an overwhelming experience. Adapting to environments that favor neurotypical behaviors has been a lifelong skill for many. These coping mechanisms often become second nature, making it challenging to recognize one's true self beneath the layers of adaptation and masking. Realizing that these behaviors were compensations for unrecognized neurodivergence can evoke emotions ranging from relief to confusion.

Let's start by examining societal and gender biases that contribute to delayed diagnoses. These prejudices delay recognition and shape how individuals perceive themselves and their struggles. As we understand the emotional landscape, we also discuss the importance of seeking support and validation from trusted sources, such as family, friends, therapists, and peer support groups. Journaling and self-reflection are valuable tools for processing complex emotions and gaining deeper insights into one's experiences. Additionally, we emphasize the role of professional guidance, mindfulness practices, and creative activities in fostering self-acceptance and authenticity. By connecting with supportive communities and setting realistic goals, individuals can navigate the unmasking journey with resilience and confidence, ultimately embracing their true selves.

Understanding the Emotional Impact of Discovering Neurodivergence Later in Life

Discovering one's neurodivergence later in life can be a profound and transformative experience. It often begins with uncovering the societal factors that contribute to late diagnoses of autism and ADHD. Our society is riddled with misconceptions and stereotypes about what it means to be neurodivergent. These biases often lead to late recognition and diagnosis, especially for adults who have spent their lives adapting and masking their differences.

Individuals with autism or ADHD often find themselves navigating environments that prioritize neurotypical behaviors. Many modern workplaces feature open-plan offices that can be overwhelming for individuals with autism or ADHD due to noise, bright lights, and constant social interaction, making it difficult for them to focus and be productive. Jobs that require multitasking, frequent changes in priorities, and strict deadlines can be particularly stressful for individuals with ADHD, who find time management and organization challenging. Neurotypical communication relies heavily on eye contact and specific body language, which can be difficult for autistic individuals who may find direct eye contact uncomfortable or misinterpret nonverbal cues. Schools, workplaces, and social settings may not accommodate or recognize the unique needs of neurodivergent individuals, leading them to develop coping mechanisms that disguise their true selves. This widespread lack of understanding and acceptance plays a significant role in why so many go undiagnosed until later in life.

In addition to societal norms, gender biases also contribute to delayed diagnoses. For example, research has shown that women are often underdiagnosed because their symptoms might present differently or be less overt compared to men. As a result, many individuals only discover their neurodivergence well into adulthood after years of feeling misunderstood and out of place.

For those who receive a late diagnosis, there is often a profound sense of relief and validation. Finally, understanding the reasons behind one's behaviors, struggles, and strengths can be incredibly empowering. This new self-awareness allows individuals to make sense of their past experiences and see themselves in a new light. The pieces of a lifelong puzzle start to fit together, providing clarity and insight into personal identity.

This sense of validation can bring immense comfort. Knowing one is not alone and that others share experiences within the neurodivergent community fosters a sense of belonging and acceptance. This newfound understanding encourages individuals to embrace their authentic selves, affirming their worth and uniqueness.

However, this wave of relief is often accompanied by mixed emotions. It's not uncommon for individuals to initially react with shock, denial, and disbelief upon receiving a late diagnosis. These reactions stem from a lifetime of internalizing societal expectations and a sense of normalcy built around masking behaviors. Accepting a new label can feel daunting and disruptive to one's self-perception.

Feelings of denial may surface as the individual grapples with the idea that they have been living with an unrecognized condition for so long. This disbelief can be compounded by questioning how life might have been different had they known earlier. The initial phase post-diagnosis can be emotionally turbulent as individuals navigate through varying feelings of confusion, frustration, and grief.

It is crucial to seek support and validation from trusted sources during this vulnerable period. Whether it's family members, friends, therapists, or peer support groups, connecting with those who understand and offer empathy can make a significant difference. Sharing experiences and emotions with others who have walked similar paths provides reassurance and solidarity, aiding in the acceptance process.

One effective tool for processing these complex emotions is journaling. Writing down thoughts, feelings, and reflections allows individuals to articulate and explore their inner world. Journaling serves as a therapeutic outlet, helping to clarify confusing emotions and track progress over time. It promotes self-awareness and helps individuals gain deeper insights into their own experiences.

Self-reflection, paired with journaling, further aids in emotional processing. Reflecting on daily interactions, triggers, and personal growth moments enables individuals to connect more deeply with their neurodivergent identity. This practice encourages mindfulness and fosters a greater understanding of how past masking behaviors influenced their lives.

In addition to self-reflection, seeking therapy or counseling can offer guidance and support during this developmental period. Therapists experienced with neurodiversity provide valuable tools and strategies for coping with the revelation of a late diagnosis. Counseling sessions can create a safe space to discuss emotions, challenges, and ways to integrate this new aspect of identity into daily life.

Connecting with peer support groups or online communities is another essential strategy for coping. These groups offer a forum to meet and exchange stories, advice, and encouragement from others who have experienced similar journeys. Finding a supportive community promotes a sense of belonging and minimizes feelings of isolation, making the unmasking process less daunting.

Embracing One's Authentic Self Post-Diagnosis

Embracing one's authentic self post-diagnosis can be a transformative experience. For many, it involves recognizing personal strengths and unique traits as part of their neurodivergent identity. Understanding and valuing these traits can lead to a more positive self-concept and increased self-esteem. Individuals diagnosed later in life often have a wealth of experiences that reveal innate strengths and qualities when viewed through the lens of their diagnosis. For example, someone might discover that their intense focus on particular subjects manifests their neurodivergence and a unique strength they bring to their interests and work.

Acknowledging these traits allows one to embrace previously misunderstood or undervalued qualities. For instance, an autistic person's ability to notice details others might miss can be seen as a valuable skill rather than a quirk. By reframing such traits positively, individuals can build a foundation of self-acceptance and pride in their neurodivergent identity. This acceptance is crucial for unmasking because it enables individuals to feel comfortable expressing their true selves without fear of judgment or rejection.

Developing this recognition also involves reflecting on past experiences and identifying moments of resilience and adaptability. Such reflections can highlight personal growth and the ability to thrive despite challenges, reinforcing that one's neurodivergent traits are not just aspects to be managed but integral parts of a strong and capable individual. Recognizing personal strengths helps form a balanced view of oneself, fostering a sense of authenticity and empowerment.

Communicating with loved ones openly and honestly about neurodivergence and unmasking is another essential step in embracing one's authentic self. Open communication helps build understanding and support among family members and friends. When neurodivergent individuals share their experiences and feelings, it can demystify behaviors that may have previously been puzzling or misinterpreted by loved ones. This honesty opens the door to deeper connections and mutual respect.

Honest discussions can also lead to setting realistic expectations within relationships. Loved ones who understand the reasons behind certain behaviors are more likely to respond with empathy and patience. This understanding creates a supportive environment where the neurodivergent person feels safe to be themselves. It is essential, however, to approach these conversations with sensitivity, providing loved ones with the information they need to understand without overwhelming them.

Moreover, communication is a two-way street. Encouraging questions and being open to discussions about neurodivergence can foster a continuous dialogue that evolves with time. As both parties learn and grow, the relationship can become a source of growth and comfort, helping the neurodivergent individual maintain their commitment to living authentically.

Exploring interests and passions that align with one's authentic self is a rewarding aspect of the unmasking journey. Engaging in special interests can be a powerful way to express one's true identity. These pursuits provide a sense of purpose and joy, allowing individuals to showcase their talents and skills in environments where they feel most comfortable and competent.

Many neurodivergent individuals have deep, specific interests that bring them immense satisfaction. Embracing these passions can lead to new opportunities for self-expression and social connection. Whether joining a club, taking a class, or simply dedicating time to a beloved hobby, these activities can inspire creativity and enthusiasm. They offer a break from daily stresses and contribute positively to mental well-being.

Furthermore, pursuing authentic interests can introduce neurodivergent individuals to like-minded people, fostering a sense of community and belonging. Finding spaces where one's uniqueness is celebrated rather than merely tolerated can reinforce the comfort and confidence needed to fully embrace an authentic lifestyle.

Reflecting on personal growth and moments of courage in the unmasking journey is vital for maintaining motivation and perspective. Each step taken towards living more authentically represents progress, no matter how small. Celebrating these milestones can boost morale and provide tangible evidence of strength and capability.

Personal reflection allows individuals to acknowledge the difficulties they've overcome and the strategies that have worked for them. Keeping a journal or creating a visual record of achievements can serve as a reminder of personal evolution and resilience. Looking back at these records during challenging times can reignite determination and hope, reminding individuals of their ability to persevere.

Additionally, reflecting on growth encourages individuals to set new goals and aspirations. Recognizing how far they've come can inspire confidence in their ability to face future challenges. It's an ongoing process of self-discovery and improvement, where each courageous act contributes to building a life that genuinely reflects who they are.

Incorporating these elements into daily life requires dedication and mindfulness but leads to a more fulfilling existence. Self-care and self-compassion are fundamental in fostering resilience amidst challenges. It's essential to take time for activities that nourish the mind and body, whether through relaxation techniques, exercise, or pursuing creative outlets.

Setting boundaries and asserting individual needs in relationships are equally important. Ensuring that interactions with others are respectful of one's neurodiverse identity helps maintain a healthy balance. This might involve explaining sensory sensitivities, requesting accommodations, or communicating preferences clearly.

Nurturing genuine connections and celebrating authenticity and mutual understanding further aids in integrating unmasking into everyday life. Being surrounded by supportive, empathetic individuals makes a significant difference in maintaining one's commitment to living authentically. These relationships buffer against external pressures to conform and provide encouragement and validation.

Finally, setting achievable goals for gradual unmasking and self-expression helps sustain momentum. Breaking down larger objectives into manageable steps ensures steady progress while preventing overwhelm. Celebrating even small victories reinforces the positive impact of unmasking, encouraging continued growth and exploration of one's true self.

Coping with Challenges and Embracing Authenticity

Including mindfulness techniques to manage stress and anxiety during the unmasking process can be transformative for those receiving a late autism or ADHD diagnosis. Mindfulness helps increase awareness of one's thoughts, feelings, and surroundings without judgment, which is crucial during the overwhelming unmasking process. Simple practices, such as deep breathing exercises, progressive muscle relaxation, or mindful walking, can help bring calmness and clarity. For example, a few minutes of deep breathing each morning can significantly reduce anxiety.

Try this:

1. Exhale through your mouth to make a whooshing sound.

2. Inhale slowly through your nose.

3. Hold your breath for several seconds.

4. Exhale slowly through your mouth.

This routine allows individuals to start their day with tranquility, making it easier to cope with daily challenges.

In addition to specific exercises, integrating mindfulness into everyday activities can enhance emotional regulation. Paying close attention to mundane tasks like eating or brushing teeth can turn these moments into opportunities for grounding oneself in the present. This approach reduces the tendency to ruminate on past mistakes or future worries, which often exacerbate stress and anxiety. Furthermore, several apps and online resources offer guided mindfulness sessions tailored to varying needs and preferences, making mindfulness accessible to everyone. Incorporating these tools into a daily routine can provide ongoing support during the unmasking journey.

Mindfulness also promotes self-compassion, which is essential for embracing authenticity. By practicing non-judgmental awareness, individuals can learn to accept their neurodivergent traits without self-criticism. Writing kind notes to oneself or recalling daily gratitude can foster a gentle attitude toward personal growth. Over time, this shift in mindset can help dissolve the internalized stigma associated with autism or ADHD, allowing individuals to unmask confidently and authentically.

Engaging in creative activities that reflect personal values and interests is another effective strategy in the unmasking process. Creative projects provide a safe space to explore and express one's authentic self, free from societal expectations. Activities such as painting, writing, music, or gardening can become powerful tools for self-discovery and expression. For instance, journaling allows individuals to process their thoughts and emotions, providing insight into their true selves. This practice encourages introspection and helps them articulate their experiences better.

Participation in creative groups or clubs can also offer a sense of community and belonging, vital for mental well-being. Joining an art class or a book club can connect like-minded individuals with similar interests, fostering a supportive environment. These collaborations can lead to meaningful friendships and provide opportunities to share personal experiences, further validating one's identity. Additionally, publicly showcasing one's creative work, whether through exhibitions, social media, or performances, can be empowering and affirming.

Moreover, creative activities can serve as a form of therapeutic intervention. Art therapy, for example, uses creative expression to improve mental health and emotional resilience. Engaging in regular creative practices not only helps in managing stress but also strengthens one's sense of self. Through art, individuals can externalize and make sense of complex emotions related to their diagnosis, turning possibly harmful experiences into opportunities for growth and healing.

Finding a therapist experienced in working with neurodivergent individuals and late diagnoses is critical for navigating the complexities of unmasking. A specialized therapist can offer personalized strategies that address the unique challenges faced during this process. They can provide cognitive-behavioral techniques, such as reframing negative thoughts or developing coping mechanisms tailored to the individual's needs. This personalized approach ensures that the unmasking journey is manageable and supported.

Therapists can also facilitate group therapy sessions where individuals with relatable experiences come together to share and learn from each other. This group dynamic provides mutual support and reduces feelings of isolation. Hearing others' stories and insights can be incredibly validating and motivating, helping individuals feel understood and less alone. Group therapy can also introduce new perspectives and strategies that one might not encounter in individual sessions.

A trusting relationship with a mental health professional is essential for effective therapy. Trust enables open communication and honesty, allowing individuals to express their fears, hopes, and experiences without hesitation. Regular sessions with a compassionate and knowledgeable therapist create a safe space for exploring one's identity and addressing any trauma or negative experiences related to masking. Over time, this therapeutic relationship becomes a cornerstone of emotional support, guiding the person through their unmasking journey with encouragement and understanding.

Setting realistic goals and expectations for personal growth and unmasking is fundamental for long-term success and well-being. Unrealistic expectations can accompany frustration and disappointment, whereas achievable goals promote steady progress and confidence. It's essential to break down larger objectives into smaller, manageable steps. For instance, if the goal is to communicate more openly about one's diagnosis, one might start by sharing this information with a trusted friend or family member before gradually expanding to broader social circles.

Consistently reviewing and adjusting these goals is also necessary. Personal growth is not a linear process; there will be setbacks and achievements along the way. Regularly reflecting on what has been accomplished and what still needs attention helps maintain a balanced perspective. This practice involves celebrating small victories and learning from challenges without harsh self-criticism. Tools like progress journals or vision boards can visually track and inspire continual development.

The Journey of Self-Discovery and Personal Growth

Embracing the process of unmasking after a late diagnosis of autism or ADHD is a profound journey of self-discovery and personal growth. This journey often begins with the importance of seeing oneself authentically and without masks in safe environments. Creating these secure spaces can significantly aid in shedding the protective layers built over time to fit social norms. Safe environments include close family gatherings, support groups composed of fellow neurodivergent individuals, or even virtual spaces where acceptance is the norm. These arenas provide comfort and reassurance, making revealing one's true self easier without fear of judgment or rejection.

In these safe spaces, authenticity can flourish as individuals experiment with expressing their genuine thoughts and emotions. Gradually, unmasking in familiar territories builds confidence for more public settings. Transparency with trusted friends or colleagues can foster deeper connections as they witness your authentic self. The process may be gradual but consistently practiced, leading to long-term mental and emotional well-being benefits. As you embrace your true self, remember that not every environment will be conducive to unmasking, so prioritize those that offer support and understanding.

During this transition, practicing assertiveness and boundary-setting is crucial to honoring one's needs and values. Assertiveness involves confidently expressing your preferences, desires, and limits in a way that is respectful to yourself and others. By setting clear boundaries, you communicate what is acceptable and necessary for your well-being. This practice helps protect you from overwhelming situations or interactions that could compromise your efforts toward authenticity. For example, if certain social situations are draining, declining invitations or requesting accommodations that make participation more comfortable is okay.

Setting boundaries also means prioritizing self-care and recognizing when to step back and recharge. Communication is vital in this process; clearly articulating your needs to loved ones and colleagues ensures they understand and respect your limitations. Over time, regularly practicing assertiveness and boundary-setting reinforces self-respect and teaches others how to interact with you in ways that support your journey. It's important to remember that establishing boundaries is not about pushing others away but building a framework that promotes mutual respect and healthy relationships.

Reflecting on personal growth and changes in self-perception throughout the unmasking process highlights the transformative power of this journey. Initially, there may be moments of uncertainty and self-doubt as you adjust to living more authentically. However, regular self-reflection can illuminate the progress made along the way. Journaling your experiences, for instance, can help track emotional and behavioral shifts, providing tangible evidence of growth. Reflective practices encourage an ongoing dialogue with yourself, developing a more significant understanding and appreciation of your journey.

This introspection underscores how far you've come and identifies areas needing further exploration or adjustment. Reflecting on moments of bravery, new accomplishments, and shifts in how you perceive yourself aids in solidifying a positive self-concept. Additionally, discussing insights gained through reflection with trusted allies can bring added clarity and validation. Embrace these reflections as opportunities to celebrate incremental achievements and recognize the resilience you've developed in navigating this complex path.

Recognizing the strength and resilience gained through embracing one's authentic self is vital to the unmasking journey. Every step toward authentic living is a testament to your inner fortitude and capacity to thrive despite societal pressures. Celebrate these victories, whether big or small, acknowledging the courage to dismantle long-held masks and present your true self to the world. This recognition reinforces the empowerment derived from authenticity and personal growth.

This journey's challenges enhance your resilience, preparing you to handle future obstacles with greater confidence and poise. Understanding that your experiences contribute to a stronger, more self-assured identity can be incredibly empowering. Sharing your stories of resilience with others can inspire them to embark on their own journeys of unmasking, fostering a community of support and solidarity.

Conclusion: Navigating the Path to Authenticity

Discovering one's neurodivergence later in life is a profoundly transformative experience filled with mixed emotions and self-discovery. Throughout this chapter, we have looked into the emotional impact of such a revelation, exploring how societal and gender biases can delay diagnoses and lead individuals to mask their true selves for years. We have uncovered the relief and validation that come with understanding one's behaviors, struggles, and strengths through the lens of autism or ADHD.

As we revisit the journey of unmasking, it becomes clear that embracing an authentic identity is challenging and rewarding. The process often begins with recognizing and valuing personal strengths that have long gone unappreciated. Individuals build a foundation of self-acceptance and pride by reframing these traits positively. This shift in perspective is essential for unmasking, as it allows one to express one's true self without fear of judgment.

Yet, this journey is not without its hurdles. The initial shock, denial, and disbelief reactions are common, stemming from years of internalized societal norms and masking behaviors. Accepting a new label can feel daunting and disrupt one's self-perception. These mixed emotions highlight the importance of seeking support from trusted sources, whether family, friends, therapists, or peer groups, to navigate this vulnerable period.

Mindfulness and self-reflection play crucial roles in managing the stress and anxiety linked to unmasking. Journaling offers a therapeutic outlet for articulating thoughts and tracking progress, while mindfulness techniques help maintain emotional regulation. Engaging in creative activities aligned with personal interests further fosters authenticity and provides joy and purpose.

Therapy is a significant support system, offering personalized strategies and a safe space to reflect on emotions and challenges. Therapists experienced with neurodiversity can guide individuals through the complexities of unmasking, helping them develop coping mechanisms tailored to their unique needs.

Open communication with loved ones about neurodivergence is vital for building understanding and support. Honest discussions pave the way for deeper connections and mutual respect, enabling neurodivergent individuals to set realistic expectations within relationships.

The broader implications of embracing authenticity extend beyond personal growth. As more individuals unmask and share their journeys, societal awareness and acceptance of neurodiversity can improve. This collective effort can help dismantle misconceptions and evolve into a more inclusive environment for future generations.

In reflecting on this journey, it is essential to recognize the strength and resilience gained through unmasking. Each step taken toward living authentically represents significant progress and requires immense courage. Celebrating these milestones reinforces the empowerment derived from authenticity and personal growth.

As you continue your journey, remember that embracing your true self is a continuous process. Setting achievable goals and practicing self-compassion will help sustain momentum. Reflect on how far you've come, and use these reflections to inspire confidence in facing future challenges.

Ultimately, the journey of self-discovery and individual growth after a late diagnosis of autism or ADHD is deeply personal and unique. It invites you to uncover your authentic self, embrace your strengths, and forge meaningful connections with others who understand and support your path. Embrace this journey with kindness and patience, knowing each step brings you closer to living a life that genuinely reflects who you are.

Psychological Layers: The Effects of Prolonged Masking

P rolonged masking takes a significant toll on the mental and emotional well-being of late-diagnosed autistic adults and individuals with ADHD. The act of continuously presenting a socially acceptable façade can lead to heightened anxiety and depression, which often go unspoken. The effort to maintain this mask results in increased stress and internal turmoil as individuals struggle to align their behavior with societal expectations. As the mental strain accumulates over weeks, months, or even years, it becomes harder to find peace and relax, leading to further complications in one's mental health.

Throughout this chapter, we will step into the various psychological layers affected by prolonged masking. We will explore the anxiety and depression that often accompany such behaviors, the impact on self-identity and self-worth, and the cognitive fatigue that results from continuous masking. The effects on relationships and social interactions will also be highlighted, shedding light on the challenges faced by those who mask their true selves. By understanding these complexities, readers will gain insight into the profound toll that prolonged masking takes and the importance of embracing authenticity for better mental health.

Anxiety and Depression from Prolonged Masking

Anxiety and depression are often the unspoken companions of extended periods of masking, particularly for late-diagnosed autistic adults and individuals with ADHD. This subpoint aims to uncover these mental health issues, shedding light on the emotional landscape shaped by prolonged masking behaviors.

Anxiety is a common outcome of sustained masking practices. The constant effort to present a socially acceptable persona can lead to heightened feelings of anxiety, resulting in increased stress and internal turmoil. For many, the fear of being judged or misunderstood intensifies the need to maintain this façade, creating a relentless cycle of worry and discomfort. The mental strain accumulates as days become weeks and months, making it harder to relax and find peace.

The struggle with anxiety often manifests in physical symptoms such as headaches, muscle tension, physical exhaustion, and difficulty sleeping. These symptoms become more pronounced as the internal conflict between one's authentic self and the masked persona grows. For those already prone to anxiety, the additional burden of masking exacerbates their condition, leading to more frequent and severe episodes of panic and distress. It becomes a daily battle to manage both the external demands of social interactions and the internal chaos that masking perpetuates.

Masking behaviors further complicate the experience of anxiety by compelling individuals to constantly monitor their actions, expressions, and words. This hyper-vigilance can be exhausting, leaving little room for spontaneity or genuine connection. Over time, the effort required to sustain the mask drains emotional energy, making it even more challenging to cope with everyday stressors.

Highlighting the struggle of constant masking illuminates the internal conflicts that many face. The tension between the desire to be accepted and the need to stay true to oneself creates a profound sense of unease. This struggle is particularly acute for late-diagnosed autistic adults and individuals with ADHD, who may have spent years trying to fit into societal norms while suppressing their true identities.

The internal conflict often leads to feelings of isolation and loneliness. Despite being surrounded by people, the masked individual feels disconnected because they are not fully seen or understood. This disconnection can deepen the alienation, making it challenging to seek support or express genuine emotions. The fear of revealing their true selves and facing rejection keeps many trapped in a cycle of silence and solitude.

This struggle also impacts self-esteem and self-worth. Constantly hiding one's true self can lead to feelings of inadequacy and self-doubt. Individuals may start to believe that their authentic selves are not good enough, reinforcing negative self-perceptions. This diminished self-esteem makes it even more challenging to break free from masking behaviors, perpetuating the cycle of internal conflict and emotional distress.

Coping mechanisms are essential for managing anxiety symptoms related to masking. One effective strategy is practicing mindfulness, which helps individuals stay present and reduce the mental chatter associated with anxiety. Mindfulness practices, such as focused breathing and meditation, can provide a temporary respite from the pressure of masking, allowing individuals to reconnect with their inner selves.

Another valuable approach is seeking therapy or counseling. Professional guidance can offer new viewpoints and coping strategies tailored to each individual's needs. Therapists can help identify triggers and develop personalized plans to manage anxiety, providing a supportive space to explore thoughts and emotions without judgment. Group therapy can also be beneficial, connecting individuals facing similar struggles and providing a sense of community and shared understanding.

Establishing a network of friends and family is also crucial for support. Sharing experiences with trusted loved ones can alleviate some emotional burdens, offering validation and encouragement. Open communication about the challenges of masking can strengthen relationships and increase feelings of acceptance and belonging. Encouraging others to understand and accept one's authentic self can create a safer environment for gradual unmasking.

Depression effects are another significant consequence of continual masking. The emotional exhaustion that accompanies prolonged efforts to conform to societal expectations can lead to depressive tendencies. This type of depression is often characterized by a pervasive sense of hopelessness and a loss of interest in previously enjoyed activities. The constant emotional labor takes a toll, draining the joy and enthusiasm from daily life.

The link between prolonged masking and depression can be attributed to the persistent suppression of one's true identity. When individuals consistently hide their authentic selves, they may lose touch with what genuinely brings them happiness and fulfillment. This disconnection from their desires and passions contributes to a growing emptiness and despair. Without outlets for genuine self-expression, the monotony of masking can make life feel dull and purposeless.

Additionally, the energy expended on maintaining the mask leaves little room for self-care and relaxation. Over time, this neglect of personal well-being exacerbates depressive symptoms. Individuals may find themselves caught in a cycle of low mood and low energy, struggling to muster the motivation to engage in activities that could improve their mental health. The longer this cycle continues, the harder it becomes to break free, deepening the severity of depression.

The emotional exhaustion resulting from continual masking also affects physical health. Chronic stress and emotional strain weaken the immune system, making individuals more susceptible to illnesses. The body's response to prolonged stress includes increased production of cortisol, leading to various health issues, including inflammation. This physical decline further reinforces the depressive state, creating a feedback loop where poor health exacerbates depression and vice versa.

Impact on Self-Identity and Self-Worth

Long-term masking can gradually distort one's self-identity. Individuals often lose touch with their true selves by presenting a façade to fit social expectations. This disconnect grows as the boundary between the masked persona and genuine identity blurs. People might be influenced by the traits they adopt to blend in, leading to a skewed perception of who they are.

This distortion of self-perception is particularly challenging for those diagnosed with autism or ADHD later in life. Many have spent years trying to conform to typical societal norms, denying parts of their natural selves. Over time, this suppression can create an internal conflict, challenging distinguishing between learned behaviors and innate characteristics. The divergence between the true self and the adopted persona creates confusion and a sense of disconnection.

Moreover, continuous masking can lead individuals to internalize negative feedback from others, further complicating self-perception. They may start believing in the criticism directed at their masked personas, influencing their views on their worth and capabilities. Such prolonged distortion impacts personal growth and emotional well-being, making embracing one's true identity more arduous.

An identity crisis often emerges from the tension between the masked persona and the authentic self. Individuals who constantly mask their true selves might feel like they are living dual lives, fostering insecurity and instability. This internal battle can be exhausting, as maintaining a façade requires continuous effort and vigilance.

The conflicting personas can lead to feelings of alienation and loneliness. Friends and family might know only the masked version, leaving the individual feeling misunderstood and isolated. This divide deepens the emotional chasm, bridging the gap between the two identities even harder. Understanding that the masked persona isn't genuinely accepted, people might withdraw further, exacerbating the identity crisis.

Navigating through this crisis demands significant introspection and courage. Individuals must recognize the necessity of unmasking to align their external behavior with their true inner selves. Support groups, therapy, and reflective practices can aid in addressing these conflicts, helping to integrate fragmented aspects of their identity and move towards wholeness.

Rebuilding one's identity after years of masking involves rediscovering and reaffirming the true self. This process begins with self-reflection, understanding past choices, and distinguishing them from intrinsic desires. Individuals need to explore their genuine interests, values, and strengths without the influence of societal pressures.

Engaging in activities that resonate with their valid preferences is a vital step in this journey. Whether it's pursuing hobbies, joining like-minded communities, or simply spending time in reflective solitude, these actions help solidify the sense of self. Journaling, creative expression, and mindfulness practices provide avenues for reconnecting with one's core identity.

Seeking professional support, like therapy, can offer structured strategies and insights to facilitate this rebuilding process. Therapists can guide individuals through exercises designed to dismantle long-held façades and foster self-acceptance. Gradual exposure to environments where unmasking feels safe encourages authenticity, leading to a more coherent and genuine sense of self.

Self-worth erosion is another significant consequence of prolonged masking. Consistently hiding true feelings or behaviors to meet external standards can diminish one's sense of value. Self-esteem suffers a severe blow when validation comes solely from how well one conforms rather than who one genuinely is

The constant comparison with others' expectations fosters a sense of inadequacy. Individuals begin to believe that their authentic selves aren't good enough, perpetuating a cycle of self-doubt and low self-esteem. Over time, this eroded sense of self-worth affects various life aspects, including relationships, career ambitions, and overall mental health.

Recognizing this erosion is the first step toward healing. Individuals can take proactive steps towards rebuilding confidence by acknowledging the negative impact of masking on their self-worth. This involves celebrating small triumphs, recognizing natural strengths, and pursuing supportive environments that appreciate authenticity over conformity.

It's crucial to employ strategies focusing on internal validation and self-acceptance. One practical guideline is to prioritize self-affirmation practices. Daily affirmations can reinforce positive beliefs about oneself, gradually offsetting the ingrained negativity resulting from years of masking.

Self Affirming meditation focuses on cultivating compassion and love towards oneself. This practice can enhance self-acceptance by fostering a sense of kindness and compassion towards oneself.

Steps:

1. **Find a Quiet Space** : Choose a quiet and comfortable place to sit or lie down without distractions.

2. **Settle In** : Close your eyes and take a few slow breaths, allowing your body to relax. Focus on the present moment.

3. **Visualize yourself in your mind's eye.**

   ○ Silently repeat phrases of loving-kindness towards yourself. For example:

     ▪ "May I be happy."

     ▪ "May I be healthy."

     ▪ "May I be safe."

     ▪ "May I live with ease."

   ○ As you repeat these phrases, try to truly feel the meaning of the words. If it helps, place a hand over your heart as a gesture of self-compassion.

5. **Conclude the Practice** :

   ○ Take a few slow breaths.

   ○ Reflect on the feelings of love and kindness you have cultivated.

   ○ Gently open your eyes and take a moment to reorient yourself to your surroundings.

Benefits:

- **Enhances Self-Compassion** : Fosters a kind and compassionate attitude towards oneself.

- **Reduces Negative Emotions** : Can help diminish feelings of self-criticism and judgment.

- **Promotes Emotional Well-Being** : Supports overall emotional health by promoting positive emotions.

Another valuable strategy is setting healthy boundaries. Learning to say no to situations that demand masking and yes to those that welcome authenticity empowers individuals. This conscious choice helps rebuild a sense of control and respect for one's genuine self, enhancing self-worth and emotional resilience.

Lastly, engaging with supportive communities plays a pivotal role. Finding spaces where one can be unapologetically authentic provides much-needed validation and acceptance. These environments act as safe havens, encouraging individuals to accept their authentic selves without fear of judgment and fostering a renewed sense of self-worth.

It's paramount for individuals to embark on an authentic journey to reclaim their true selves. This journey involves shedding the layers of accumulated masks and embracing one's inherent traits and quirks. It's about finding joy in being unapologetically oneself and celebrating uniqueness.

A practical approach slowly introduces aspects of the authentic self into daily interactions. This gradual unmasking allows for a smoother transition and reduces the risk of overwhelming oneself with drastic changes. Celebrating moments of authenticity encourages continued efforts in this journey, reinforcing the importance of staying true to oneself.

Ultimately, the path to authenticity is ongoing and evolving. Embracing the journey requires patience, persistence, and a deep commitment to self-growth. Individuals can create a fulfilling and authentic life by regularly reflecting on progress, adjusting approaches as needed, and remaining open to new experiences.

Finding one's purpose beyond the mask is a transformative experience. This involves connecting with passions and aspirations that resonate with the true self, unhindered by societal expectations. Identifying and pursuing meaningful goals cultivates a sense of direction and fulfillment.

Exploring various interests and cultivating curiosity are essential steps in discovering purpose. Whether through volunteering, engaging in creative endeavors, or learning new skills, these activities help uncover passions that might have been suppressed due to masking. This exploration is crucial in formulating a clear sense of purpose.

Cognitive Fatigue from Continuous Masking

Cognitive fatigue from prolonged masking significantly impacts the mental and emotional health of individuals, especially those diagnosed with ADHD or late-diagnosed autism. Cognitive overload is a primary concern. Constantly masking behaviors to conform to societal expectations demands continuous mental effort. This persistent strain increases cognitive exhaustion, making it difficult for individuals to navigate social environments comfortably. For adults with ADHD, this cognitive burden manifests as heightened mental fatigue, often resulting in difficulty sustaining focus and maintaining productivity.

In social situations, cognitive overload can become overwhelming. Individuals continuously monitor their behavior, facial expressions, and tone of voice to align with perceived social norms. This constant vigilance requires significant cognitive resources, leading to rapid depletion. The mental exhaustion that follows impacts individuals' ability to engage authentically, diminishing their capacity to form genuine connections. For late-diagnosed autistic adults, this exhaustion is profoundly felt, affecting their overall mental health and sense of self.

The effects of cognitive overload extend beyond social interactions. The sustained mental effort required for masking can impact other areas of life, such as work and personal relationships. When cognitive resources are depleted, individuals may struggle with decision-making, problem-solving, and daily tasks. This all-too-common scenario underscores the importance of addressing cognitive overload as part of broader mental health and well-being strategies for individuals frequently engaging in masking behaviors.

Another aspect of cognitive fatigue is the multitasking struggle inherent in managing multiple personas simultaneously. For individuals masking their true selves, juggling different identities based on social contexts is common. This involves constantly switching between various roles and traits, which places immense cognitive demands on the brain. Late-diagnosed autistic adults often find this particularly challenging, as they may already face difficulties in flexible thinking and adapting to changing social cues.

The effort to maintain these personas can lead to cognitive fragmentation, where the individual struggles to keep each persona distinct and coherent. This mental juggling act increases the risk of errors and inconsistencies, adding to the stress and anxiety associated with masking. Over time, the brain's capacity to manage these multiple personas diminishes, resulting in feeling overwhelmed and mentally scattered. Such experiences can be disheartening and contribute to overall cognitive and emotional fatigue.

For individuals with ADHD, multitasking while masking presents unique challenges. ADHD inherently affects executive functioning skills, including planning, organization, and task management. When combined with the need to mask, these individuals may find themselves mentally overloaded more quickly, fighting to maintain internal and external demands. This ongoing battle can lead to feelings of inadequacy and frustration, further exacerbating the cognitive fatigue experienced.

Memory drain is another critical factor in the cognitive fatigue resulting from prolonged masking. The brain's cognitive resources are heavily taxed when constantly adapting to different social contexts and masking genuine emotions or traits. This can lead to significant memory issues, as the brain prioritizes immediate social survival over long-term information retention. Individuals may need to remember important details or help recall events accurately.

The impact of memory drain extends to various aspects of life. For instance, individuals may have difficulty remembering tasks, deadlines, or important meetings at work. In social settings, recalling names, conversations, or past interactions becomes challenging, affecting the ability to build and maintain relationships. This consistent cognitive load disrupts the brain's typical functioning, making it harder for individuals to stay organized and focused.

Moreover, the quality of work and social interactions may suffer due to memory drain. Individuals might experience decreased productivity, make more mistakes, or become less reliable in fulfilling commitments. The ongoing struggle with memory issues can also lead to reduced self-confidence, as individuals fear they cannot trust their recollections. This further contributes to the cycle of cognitive fatigue and emotional stress.

Addressing cognitive burnout associated with prolonged masking requires effective strategies for preventing and managing its onset. One crucial approach is practicing mindfulness. Mindfulness techniques help individuals stay grounded in the present moment, reducing the mental strain of constantly anticipating social demands. Simple practices like deep breathing exercises or short meditation sessions can provide significant relief by calming the mind and reducing anxiety.

Rest and recovery are equally important. Ensuring adequate sleep and regular daily breaks allows the brain to recharge. Participating in activities that bring exhilaration and relaxation, such as hobbies, nature walks, or listening to music, helps replenish cognitive resources. Establishing a consistent routine incorporating downtime and self-care can significantly mitigate the effects of mental fatigue.

Setting boundaries is another vital strategy. Being selective about social engagements and learning to say no when overwhelmed can preserve cognitive energy. Prioritizing quality over quantity in social interactions helps reduce the mental load of masking. Additionally, seeking environments where authenticity is encouraged and accepted fosters a sense of safety and belonging, minimizing the need for continuous masking.

Self-reflection plays a crucial role in managing cognitive burnout. Regularly assessing one's emotional and mental state helps identify early signs of fatigue. Journaling thoughts and feelings or discussing experiences with trusted friends or therapists provides an outlet for processing emotions and gaining insights into patterns of masking behavior. This internal awareness enables individuals to make informed choices about when and how to engage socially, preserving mental well-being.

Effects on Relationships and Social Interactions

Masking, concealing one's true self behind a socially acceptable façade, has profound implications on relationships and social interactions. Over time, it impacts various facets of our lives, often in challenging ways, yet also presents growth opportunities.

The first aspect to consider is social dynamics. Masking can significantly alter how we engage with others. When individuals mask, they create a barrier between their authentic selves and those around them. This can prevent the development of deep, meaningful relationships. Instead of genuine connections based on mutual understanding and shared experiences, relationships may become superficial, driven by the masked persona rather than the actual individual. Over time, this can lead to isolation and disconnection as the masked individual yearns for authenticity but feels trapped by their façade.

Furthermore, masking can disrupt social hierarchies and group dynamics. In social settings, masked individuals may struggle to navigate complex social cues and expectations, leading to misunderstandings and conflicts. For example, a person masking their anxiety might come across as aloof or uninterested, causing others to misinterpret their behavior and potentially leading to strained relationships. Additionally, the constant effort to maintain the mask can be mentally exhausting, contributing to social fatigue and reducing one's ability to engage meaningfully with others.

However, prolonged masking also offers growth opportunities. Recognizing the impact of masking on social dynamics can be a catalyst for change. It can leverage individuals to reflect on their behaviors and motivations, fostering greater self-awareness and empathy towards themselves and others. By acknowledging the challenges posed by masking, individuals can begin the journey toward unmasking, aiming to cultivate more genuine and fulfilling relationships.

Authentic communication is crucial in the process of unmasking. Genuine communication involves expressing one's true thoughts, feelings, and experiences without fear of judgment. It allows for vulnerability, essential for building trust and intimacy in relationships. When individuals communicate authentically, they create an environment where others feel safe to do the same, fostering mutual respect and understanding.

One practical guideline for promoting authentic communication is performing active listening by giving full attention to the speaker, acknowledging their perspective, and responding thoughtfully. Individuals demonstrate empathy and respect by encouraging others to open up and share their authentic selves. Another strategy is to use "I" statements, which focus on one's experiences and feelings rather than blaming or criticizing others. For example, saying, "I feel overwhelmed when I have to hide my anxiety" instead of "You make me anxious," shifts the conversation towards self-expression and away from conflict.

Moreover, setting aside time for regular, open conversations can help reinforce the habit of authentic communication. Whether through daily check-ins, weekly discussions, or dedicated times for deeper conversations, creating consistent opportunities for genuine dialogue strengthens relationships and supports the unmasking process.

Rebuilding trust in relationships damaged by masking behaviors requires intentional effort and patience. Once broken, trust can take time to restore, but it is possible with the right approach. One effective strategy is transparency. Being open about past masking behaviors and explaining their reasons can help others understand and empathize. For instance, sharing that you masked your true feelings due to fear of rejection can provide context and foster compassion.

Another essential guideline is consistency. Demonstrating reliable and predictable behavior over time helps rebuild trust.

This means being honest, following through on commitments, and consistently showing support. Trust is reinforced when individuals know they can depend on each other in words and deeds.

Additionally, rebuilding trust also requires forgiveness to play a crucial role. Both the person who masked it and those affected by it need to engage in the process of forgiveness. This involves acknowledging the hurt caused by masking behaviors, expressing genuine remorse, and working towards healing together. Forgiveness is a two-way street, requiring effort and understanding from all parties involved.

Social withdrawal is a common consequence of prolonged masking. The mental and emotional exhaustion from constantly maintaining a façade can lead individuals to retreat from social interactions altogether. This withdrawal can manifest as avoiding social gatherings, minimizing contact with friends and family, or isolating oneself completely. While withdrawing may temporarily relieve the pressures of masking, it often exacerbates feelings of loneliness and isolation in the long run.

Addressing social withdrawal involves recognizing the signs and taking proactive steps to reengage with others. It's important to start small by contacting trusted friends or participating in low-pressure social activities. Gradually increasing social interactions can help rebuild confidence and reduce the anxiety associated with unmasking. Guidance from loved ones and mental health professionals can be invaluable during this process, as they provide encouragement and advice.

Finding communities or support groups where individuals feel understood and accepted can also be beneficial. These spaces offer a sense of belonging and allow authentic self-expression without fear of judgment. Engaging in activities that align with individual interests and values can further facilitate meaningful social connections and combat the tendency to withdraw.

Conclusion and Reflections on the Effects of Prolonged Masking

In this chapter, we have explored the mental and emotional toll that prolonged masking takes on individuals, particularly those diagnosed with autism or ADHD later in life. We have discussed how anxiety and depression are often hidden companions of extended periods of masking. The effort to present a socially acceptable persona can lead to heightened anxiety and increased stress, creating cycles of worry and discomfort. Managing these emotions while sustaining a mask can be exhausting, draining emotional energy and making it challenging to connect genuinely with others.

We also examined how masking behaviors contribute to feelings of isolation and loneliness; despite being surrounded by people, those who mask often feel disconnected because their true selves remain hidden. This disconnection can deepen the alienation, making it difficult to seek support or express genuine emotions. Additionally, constantly hiding one's true self can deteriorate self-esteem and self-worth, resulting in inadequacy and self-doubt.

To cope with these challenges, mindfulness practices like deep breathing and meditation can help individuals reconnect with their inner selves and reduce anxiety. Therapy or counseling offers tailored strategies and support, enabling individuals to manage stress more effectively. Building a supportive community of friends and family is crucial, as open communication about the challenges of masking strengthens relationships and fosters acceptance.

Depression is another significant consequence of continual masking. The emotional exhaustion from conforming to societal expectations can promote hopelessness and loss of interest in previously enjoyed activities. Prolonged masking creates a sense of emptiness and despair as individuals lose touch with what truly brings them happiness.

Cognitive fatigue also plays a significant role in the toll of prolonged masking. Adapting to different social contexts demands continuous mental effort, leading to cognitive overload and exhaustion. This can affect focus, decision-making, and memory, impacting various aspects of life, such as work and personal relationships. Addressing cognitive burnout involves practicing mindfulness, ensuring adequate rest, setting boundaries, and seeking environments where authenticity is encouraged.

Prolonged masking can skew one's self-identity and self-worth. By continuously presenting a façade, individuals often lose touch with their authentic selves, creating an internal conflict between learned behaviors and innate characteristics. Rebuilding one's identity involves self-reflection, exploring genuine interests, and seeking professional support to dismantle long-held façades.

Masking also impacts relationships and social interactions. It can create barriers to meaningful connections, disrupt social dynamics, and lead to feelings of isolation. However, recognizing the effects of masking can prompt individuals to reflect and strive for more genuine relationships. Authentic communication, active listening, and transparency are crucial to rebuilding trust and fostering more profound connections.

Ultimately, embracing authenticity and shedding the layers of accumulated masks is essential for mental and emotional well-being. The journey towards unmasking requires patience, persistence, and a commitment to self-growth. Individuals can create fulfilling and meaningful lives by gradually introducing aspects of the authentic self into daily interactions and celebrating moments of authenticity.

As we conclude this chapter, it's important to remember that the path to authenticity is ongoing and evolving. Each step taken towards unmasking and embracing one's true self is a victory. The journey may be challenging, but it promises genuine connections, self-acceptance, and a deeper understanding of one's worth. Reflecting on our experiences and remaining open to new possibilities will guide us toward a more authentic and enriching life.

Strategies for Gradual Unmasking: Steps Towards Authenticity

S trategies for gradual unmasking are essential for those striving to embrace their true selves. Starting this journey can be daunting and transformative as individuals navigate the complexities of revealing aspects of their personality that have long been hidden. Creating secure and supportive environments is a fundamental component of this process. Identifying safe spaces, whether close relationships or comforting physical locations, significantly alleviates anxiety and fosters openness. It's about surrounding oneself with understanding and non-judgmental people who encourage authenticity and provide emotional validation.

Throughout the chapter, we will explore practical steps to help gradually unmask. We will look into identifying and creating supportive starting points, leveraging online communities, and the importance of practicing self-compassion. Additionally, we'll discuss the significance of setting realistic expectations, building a supportive network, and establishing boundaries. The goal is to provide the tools and strategies that make the path toward an authentic life manageable and rewarding. This chapter aims to guide you through this empowering journey, ensuring that each step forward helps you feel more connected to your true self.

Providing a Supportive Starting Point for Readers to Initiate Their Unmasking Journey

Identifying safe spaces for initial unmasking can be crucial in beginning your journey toward authenticity. These environments should feel secure, judgment-free, and supportive of your true self. It could be as simple as starting with one trusted friend or family member who has consistently shown acceptance and understanding. Evaluate your relationships to identify who among your circle offers you an emotional safe haven where you can express yourself without fear.

Creating these safe spaces also involves choosing physical locations where you feel most comfortable and relaxed. This could be your home, a favorite café, or a cozy park bench. The key is to find places that naturally ease your anxiety levels and allow for a more serene way to open up. In a supportive environment, you'll likely find it less daunting to let down your guard and start showing aspects of your true self.

It's important to note that online communities can also serve as excellent safe spaces. Many individuals find solace in virtual groups or forums where they can share their experiences anonymously while receiving support and encouragement from like-minded people. Exploring these options can offer additional layers of security and anonymity, making taking those first vulnerable steps toward authenticity easier.

Acknowledging the importance of feeling safe and validated throughout this process cannot be overstated. The journey of unmasking requires emotional vulnerability, and knowing that your feelings and experiences are acknowledged is paramount. Validation comes from recognizing your emotions and understanding that they are genuine and legitimate, which helps build confidence.

Feeling validated often stems from both internal and external sources. Internally, practicing self-validation techniques, such as positive affirmations and mindfulness exercises, can help reinforce your sense of worth.

Here's an example of a self-validation technique called "Acknowledge and Affirm."

Acknowledge and Affirm Technique

1. **Identify Your Emotion** : Start by identifying what you are feeling. It could be a specific emotion like sadness, anger, frustration, or anxiety. For example, "I am feeling anxious."

2. **Acknowledge the Emotion** : Acknowledge that it is okay to feel this way. Everyone experiences a range of emotions, a normal part of being human. For example, "It's okay to feel anxious right now."

3. **Understand the Source** : Try to understand why you are feeling this emotion. Reflect on the situation or thoughts that might have triggered this feeling. For example, "I feel anxious because I have an important presentation tomorrow."

4. **Affirm Your Experience** : Your feelings are valid and understandable given the circumstances. For example, "It makes sense that I feel anxious about the presentation. It's a big deal, and feeling nervous about it is normal."

5. **Reassure Yourself** : Provide yourself with reassurance and support. Remind yourself that you can cope with your emotions and the situation. For example, "I have prepared well for the presentation and have done similar things before successfully. I can handle this."

Sharing your thoughts and feelings with empathetic listeners who provide feedback and affirmation can further solidify this sense of validation. Remember, being heard and understood by others fosters a deeper connection to your authentic self.

Surrounding yourself with people who genuinely appreciate and respect you is equally crucial. Validation doesn't only come from grand gestures; sometimes, small acknowledgments, like a nod during a conversation or a text message checking on you, contribute significantly to your feeling of safety and emotional security.

Establishing boundaries to protect yourself during moments of vulnerability is another essential practice. Factors like setting limits on how much you share at once and deciding who gets to see different parts of your authentic self play a significant role. Boundaries act as protective measures that allow you to gradually take control of your unmasking process rather than feeling overwhelmed.

Getting comfortable with saying 'no' or 'not yet' is vital. You have every right to decide when and where to reveal more intimate details about yourself. This strategy can be beneficial when tackling curious but uninformed acquaintances who may place undue pressure on you to reveal too much too soon. Setting clear boundaries also involves openly communicating your needs and limitations, ensuring those around you understand and respect them.

Boundaries also include time management and giving yourself permission to step back if the process becomes too intense. Taking breaks to recharge emotionally and mentally can help maintain a balanced and sustainable technique for unmasking. Being kind to yourself and respecting your limits is just as crucial as sharing your authentic self with others.

Another critical strategy is seeking out understanding individuals who can provide non-judgmental spaces for expression. People who genuinely empathize with your experiences offer a compassionate ear, which can profoundly impact your willingness and ability to show your true self. Look for traits such as active listening, patience, and kindness in these individuals.

Building connections with people who share similar journeys can also bring immense comfort. Support groups, whether in-person or online, can provide a platform where mutual understanding and shared experiences create an atmosphere of acceptance. You'll find others within these circles who resonate with your struggles and cheer on your progress.

Finally, don't hesitate to reach out for professional support if needed. Therapists, particularly those specializing in neurodiversity and masking behaviors, can offer tailored strategies and tools to aid your unmasking journey. Professional guidance ensures you aren't navigating this path alone and provides expert insights into managing challenges and celebrating milestones effectively.

Setting Realistic Expectations and Achievable Goals During the Unmasking Process

Maintaining realistic expectations and goals is essential to unmasking and embracing one's authentic self. Managing expectations starts with understanding that unmasking is a gradual process; it cannot happen overnight. By breaking down this overarching goal into smaller, manageable steps, individuals can better navigate the path to authenticity without feeling overwhelmed. For instance, instead of aiming to reveal your true self in all social settings immediately, start by being more open in safe, supportive environments. This phased approach makes the process less daunting and more achievable.

Setting realistic goals involves recognizing one's limitations and working within them. It's essential to be specific about what you want to achieve. For example, rather than having a vague objective like "be more authentic," define clear actions like "share my opinions more often in team meetings" or "spend 30 minutes daily reflecting on my true feelings." By being specific, you create tangible targets that are easier to pursue and measure. Moreover, setting time-bound milestones helps maintain focus and motivation throughout the process.

It's vital to remain flexible and adjust goals as needed. Authenticity is deeply personal, and the path to achieving it is not linear. Some days might feel more challenging than others, and that's perfectly okay. Being open to revisiting and tweaking your goals ensures they remain relevant and attainable. This adaptability prevents discouragement when progress feels slow and keeps the journey toward authenticity steady and forward-moving.

Emphasizing patience and self-compassion is equally essential during the unmasking process. Embracing authenticity requires time, and expecting immediate results can lead to frustration and disappointment. It's necessary to acknowledge that setbacks and struggles are part of the journey. Cultivating patience means allowing yourself to move at your own pace and recognizing that each small step brings you closer to your goal (Success, T., n.d.).

Self-compassion plays a pivotal role in maintaining emotional well-being throughout this journey. Offer yourself with the same grace and understanding that you would give a friend going through a similar experience. Remind yourself that having tough days and moments of doubt is okay. This gentle approach encourages resilience and makes the process of unmasking less stressful. Reflective practices like meditation or positive affirmations can reinforce self-compassion, providing a mental buffer against challenges.

Celebrating small victories along the way also bolsters patience and self-compassion. Recognize and appreciate your progress, no matter how minor it may seem. Whether you find the courage to express your genuine thoughts or resist the urge to mask in a difficult situation, these achievements signify growth. Celebrating these milestones fuels motivation and reinforces the belief that you can embrace your authentic self.

Setting small, attainable goals is another effective strategy for tracking progress and celebrating achievements. Breaking down larger objectives into smaller tasks makes the unmasking process more manageable and less intimidating.

For example, if your goal is to be more open about your neurodivergence with friends, start by sharing with one trusted person. Once you feel comfortable, gradually expand this circle. These incremental steps build confidence and make the overall goal seem more reachable.

Tracking progress through these smaller goals allows for continuous reflection and adjustment. Write down your goals, breakthroughs, and the emotions experienced along the way. This practice documents your progress and provides an outlet for processing feelings and reinforcing positive changes.

Recognizing achievements, no matter how small, is crucial in maintaining momentum. Reward yourself for the efforts you put into unmasking and the courage it takes to be your true self. These rewards don't need to be extravagant; simple acts of self-care or doing something you enjoy can serve as meaningful acknowledgments of your progress. Recognizing these moments of success reinforces the value of your journey and encourages further steps towards authenticity.

Utilizing tools like journaling or self-reflection can significantly aid in monitoring emotional and mental well-being throughout the unmasking process (MindTools | Home www.mindtools.com. , n.d.). Journals provide a private space to explore and understand your experiences and emotions. Writing about your day-to-day life, challenges faced, and moments of authenticity helps clarify your thoughts and feelings. This reflective practice can highlight patterns in your behavior and elucidate triggers that cause masking.

Self-reflection goes hand in hand with journaling. Regularly thinking about your actions and their alignment with your true self can provide valuable insights. Ask yourself questions like

"What situations make me feel most authentic?" and "Where do I still need to mask?" Answering these questions helps you understand your progress and identify areas needing more attention.

Furthermore, engaging in regular self-assessment allows for real-time adjustments in your approach. If you notice that specific environments or interactions consistently trigger masking behaviors, you can develop better strategies to handle these situations. This ongoing process of self-awareness and adjustment ensures that your journey toward authenticity remains dynamic and responsive to your needs.

Building a Supportive Network for Encouragement and Guidance During Unmasking

Building a supportive network is crucial during the gradual unmasking process. Cultivating connections with like-minded individuals who understand and champion one's authentic self can provide a strong foundation for this journey. Online support networks, such as social media groups or forums, offer a space to share experiences and gain encouragement from others walking a similar path. These communities allow for the exchange of practical advice and emotional support, creating a sense of belonging.

Offline networks also play an essential role in fostering authenticity. Joining local community activities and clubs or attending meetups related to personal interests can help form meaningful connections. These interactions provide opportunities for genuine self-expression in a safe environment. Additionally, participating in therapy sessions either individually or in groups can offer structured support and professional guidance. Therapy provides tools to navigate the emotional complexities of unmasking and helps build resilience.

Finding mentors or guides who have experience with unmasking can be particularly beneficial. A mentor can offer wisdom, share their journey, and provide tailored advice based on their experiences. This relationship often brings a deeper understanding of the challenges ahead, reassuring that authenticity is achievable. Regular check-ins with a mentor can maintain motivation and provide a source of accountability, ensuring that progress continues even when the process feels daunting.

Exploring online communities or support groups focused on unmasking and authenticity can vastly expand one's support system. These digital spaces are often filled with resources, discussions, and shared experiences, which can be incredibly validating. Joining these groups can help individuals find answers to specific questions and discover new strategies for embracing their true selves. It also allows for anonymity, making it easier for some to open up and seek help without fear of judgment.

The diversity within online communities means that there is likely a group that aligns perfectly with one's needs and identity. Whether it's a forum dedicated to autistic adults or a Facebook group for individuals with ADHD, these virtual spaces offer specialized support. The vast range of perspectives and advice available can help navigate the unique aspects of unmasking relevant to different conditions or circumstances. Engaging actively in these communities by sharing personal stories and offering support to others can create a reciprocal cycle of encouragement.

It's essential to approach online communities with discernment. Not all advice may be applicable or helpful, and it is crucial to identify positive and constructive spaces. Seeking out groups with clear guidelines for respectful interaction and moderation can ensure a more supportive experience. Healthy online communities will foster a sense of safety and mutual respect, making them valuable allies in the journey toward authenticity.

In addition to online communities, offline activities or therapy sessions can significantly aid the unmasking process. Offline activities such as hobby groups, sports teams, or creative classes provide tangible opportunities for socialization and self-expression. These settings encourage participants to showcase their passions and talents, naturally leading to a more authentic presence. Being surrounded by people with common interests creates a comfortable atmosphere where masks are less likely necessary.

Therapy sessions, whether individual or group, are another powerful tool. An experienced therapist can steer individuals through the complexities of unmasking, helping them explore underlying fears and patterns of behavior. Therapy offers a confidential space to express vulnerabilities and work through emotions tied to unmasking. Group therapy provides peer support, allowing individuals to join others facing similar challenges and learn from their journeys.

Engaging in pursuits that promote vulnerability, such as art therapy or drama workshops, can also be beneficial. These therapeutic environments encourage deep self-exploration and create greater emotional openness. By practicing vulnerability in controlled, supportive settings, individuals can gradually build the confidence to express their true selves in broader social contexts. This process of incremental exposure strengthens authenticity over time.

Seeking mentors or guides with unmasking experience is a strategic step in building a supportive network. Mentors bring a wealth of knowledge and personal insights that can illuminate the path to authenticity. Their real-life experiences provide practical examples of how to navigate the highs and lows of the unmasking journey. Having someone to turn to for advice and encouragement can alleviate isolation and uncertainty.

Mentorship relationships can take various forms, from formal coaching arrangements to informal friendships. Finding a mentor involves looking for someone whose journey resonates personally and who exhibits qualities one admires and aspires to develop. Establishing clear expectations and regular communication can maximize the benefits of the mentorship. These interactions provide a steady source of motivation and perspective, essential for maintaining momentum.

Practicing Self-Compassion and Kindness Throughout the Unmasking Process

Embracing the journey towards authenticity begins with practicing self-compassion. For many late-diagnosed autistic adults and individuals with ADHD, unmasking can be a daunting process filled with moments of vulnerability.

Cultivating a gentle and understanding attitude toward oneself is crucial during these times. Self-compassion involves recognizing that experiencing difficulties while trying to unmask is a normal part of the journey. It's about treating yourself with the kindness you would offer a loved one against similar obstacles.

One effective way to practice self-compassion is by acknowledging your feelings without judgment. If you struggle, remind yourself that feeling this way is okay. Everyone has moments of doubt and fear; these emotions don't define your worth or capability. Embrace the discomfort as a signal of growth rather than a setback. Journaling can be a therapeutic tool, allowing you to openly express your thoughts and emotions and providing a safe space for self-reflection and compassion. Remember that journaling does not necessarily need to be just words; sometimes, a picture or a doodle is enough to capture the moment's emotions. Sometimes, words don't come readily to mind, but an image can convey everything.

Additionally, self-compassion can manifest in practical ways, such as taking breaks when needed or engaging in activities that bring happiness and relaxation. Listening to your body and mind and responding lovingly to their needs is paramount. Whether engaging in quality time with loved ones, indulging in a hobby, or simply resting, these acts of kindness toward yourself reinforce the message that you deserve care and attention.

Embracing imperfections and setbacks is another crucial component of the unmasking journey. The path to authenticity is rarely linear, and accepting this reality can help alleviate unnecessary pressure. Each mistake or challenge encountered is an opportunity for learning and personal growth. Instead of viewing imperfections as failures, consider them integral building blocks of your unique story.

Understanding that setbacks are a natural part of any transformative process can shift your perspective from frustration to acceptance. Rather than focusing on the end goal, appreciate the progress made. Celebrating small victories reinforces a positive mindset and helps maintain motivation. Remember, perfection is an illusion; embracing your flaws makes you more relatable and human.

Moreover, sharing your experiences of imperfection with others can allow for a sense of community and understanding. Many individuals face similar struggles, and discussing can create a supportive network where everyone feels less alone. Authentic connections are built on shared realities, not on portraying an idealized version of oneself.

Incorporating self-care practices into your daily schedule is vital for mental and emotional well-being during the unmasking process. Prioritizing self-care helps manage stress and maintain balance. This can include mindfulness meditation, regular exercise, healthy eating, and sufficient sleep. These practices nurture the body and mind, creating a foundation of stability from which you can explore your authentic self.

Mindfulness meditation encourages present-moment awareness, allowing you to note your thoughts and emotions without attachment or judgment. This practice cultivates inner peace and resilience, making it easier to navigate challenging situations. Similarly, physical activities like yoga or walking can release tension and promote overall well-being.

Engaging in creative outlets can also be incredibly therapeutic. Whether painting, writing, music, or crafting, creative pursuits offer a form of expression that transcends verbal communication. They provide an avenue to connect with your innermost feelings and articulate them in a tangible form. Incorporating these self-care practices supports your mental health and empowers you to face the unmasking journey with renewed strength.

Recognizing and celebrating personal growth and resilience achieved through unmasking efforts is equally important. Acknowledging how far you've come fosters a sense of accomplishment and boosts your confidence. Take time to reflect on the milestones you've reached, no matter how insignificant they may seem. Each step towards authenticity is significant and deserves recognition.

Documenting your progression can be a powerful motivator. Keeping a visual representation of your achievements helps you see the cumulative impact of your efforts. Reflecting on these records during moments of doubt can reignite your determination and remind you of your capabilities.

Furthermore, sharing your successes with trusted friends or support groups can enhance your sense of achievement. Positive reinforcement from others can affirm your journey and inspire continued perseverance. Celebrating together builds a solid support system, reinforcing the communal aspect of the unmasking process.

Conclusion

Unmasking and embracing your authentic self is a profound journey that starts with creating safe spaces to be true to yourself. Throughout this chapter, we've explored various strategies to help identify these areas, recognize the importance of validation, establish boundaries, and find supportive online and offline communities. By taking gradual steps, you begin to unmask in environments that foster safety and acceptance, allowing you to test the waters of authenticity without feeling overwhelmed.

Reflecting on these points, it's clear that the unmasking process isn't about rushing into complete openness but rather about finding comfort in small, manageable steps. Starting with one trusted person or a familiar setting can ease the anxiety associated with revealing parts of yourself that you've hidden for so long. Whether it involves confiding in a close friend or joining an online forum where you feel understood, these initial actions build a foundation for further progress.

Taking time for self-compassion and kindness is crucial as you navigate through moments of vulnerability. Unmasking doesn't come without its challenges—there will be days when it feels like two steps forward and one step back. Recognizing these setbacks not as failures but as natural parts of the journey is vital. Allow yourself the grace to absorb the knowledge and grow from each experience, and remember that everyone's path to authenticity looks different.

Some readers might worry about the implications of unmasking, fearing judgment or misunderstanding from others. These concerns are valid and reflect the profoundly personal nature of this journey. However, weighing these fears against the potential consequences of continuing to mask is essential. Prolonged masking can lead to emotional exhaustion, a diminished sense of self, and even mental health issues. By gradually peeling back the layers, you allow yourself to live more genuinely and create deeper connections with those around you.

On a broader scale, increasing awareness and acceptance of neurodiversity benefits society. As more people authentically express themselves, it fosters a culture of inclusivity and understanding. This collective shift can reduce stigma and empower others hesitant to start their unmasking journey. It's a ripple effect that begins with individual courage and resonates with the broader community, paving the way for future generations to embrace their true selves.

Ending with reflective thought, consider how each small step towards authenticity contributes to a more prosperous, more fulfilling life. The journey may be ongoing, but every moment spent being true to who you are brings you closer to a place of genuine happiness and connection. What new possibilities could unfold if you continue to embrace your authentic self? What impact could your journey have on those around you, inspiring them to embark on their own paths toward authenticity?

Inner Child Healing: Reconnecting with Your True Self

I nner child healing is a powerful practice that has great potential for late-diagnosed autistic adults and individuals with ADHD. People with autism may be more vulnerable to traumatic experiences due to their unique challenges and sensitivities. Addressing this vulnerability through trauma-informed care, supportive environments, and appropriate therapeutic interventions is crucial for promoting the well-being of autistic individuals. Reconnecting with your inner child involves acknowledging the part of yourself that holds the emotions, experiences, and memories from your early years. This reconnection is not just about reminiscing; it's about uncovering hidden emotions and unresolved conflicts that have shaped who you are today. Engaging with this younger self can lead to profound healing and self-discovery, essential for embracing your true identity.

This chapter will explore how childhood experiences shape our present behaviors, emotional responses, and self-perceptions. You'll learn about therapeutic techniques like guided visualization and journaling that can help comfort and nurture your inner child. We will also explore embracing vulnerability as a pathway to inner strength and resilience, allowing for more profound self-acceptance and authentic living. By reflecting on specific memories and understanding their impact, you'll gain valuable insights into current patterns and challenges in your life, setting the stage for meaningful change and growth.

Introduction to Inner Child Work

Inner child work is a profoundly transformative practice that can guide late-diagnosed autistic adults and individuals with ADHD toward embracing their true selves. Understanding this process begins with recognizing the enduring presence of our inner child—a part of us that retains the feelings, experiences, and memories from our early years. By reconnecting with this inner child, individuals can start to uncover layers of hidden emotions and unresolved conflicts, leading to profound healing and self-discovery.

One significant aspect of inner child work is understanding how our childhood experiences shape who we are today. The inner child carries the imprints of these early experiences, both positive and negative. These memories influence our present behaviors, emotional responses, and self-perceptions. For example, a child who felt unsupported or misunderstood may grow into an adult who struggles with self-esteem or trusts others. Recognizing these connections helps us understand the root of specific patterns and challenges, providing valuable insights into our mental and emotional state.

Healing through reconnection involves the cathartic process of acknowledging and nurturing your inner child. This means embracing those parts of yourself that were wounded or neglected and offering them the care and compassion they didn't receive in the past. This reconnection is often facilitated through therapeutic techniques such as guided visualization, where you imagine comforting your younger self or writing letters to your inner child to express love and understanding. These practices help release buried emotions and foster a sense of integration and wholeness.

Embracing vulnerability is another crucial element in the journey towards authenticity. Often, our protective mechanisms—developed as children to cope with pain or fear—prevent us from being truly open and vulnerable as adults. However, by allowing ourselves to be vulnerable, we heal old wounds and build genuine connections with others. Vulnerability is not a sign of weakness but a pathway to inner strength and resilience. When we accept and express our vulnerabilities, we create space for more profound self-acceptance and authentic living.

Recognizing the role of childhood experiences in shaping our current selves can be enlightening. Reflecting on specific memories and their associated emotions can reveal patterns that explain present-day behaviors. For instance, if a person remembers feeling overlooked or dismissed by caregivers, they might realize how this impacts their need for validation in adulthood. Understanding these links empowers us to change maladaptive behaviors and replace them with healthier ones.

Reconnecting with your inner child requires patience and persistence. It is a nurturing process where you offer the love and support that was perhaps missing during your formative years. Engaging in activities you loved as a child, such as drawing or playing, can help reignite that connection. Moreover, seeking therapy or joining support groups with others undergoing similar journeys can provide additional guidance and encouragement.

Healing through reconnection also emphasizes creating a safe internal environment where your inner child feels seen and heard. This involves regular self-reflection and self-care practices. Techniques such as mindfulness meditation can help quiet the mind, allowing you to listen to your inner child's needs. These practices reinforce the idea that you are both capable and deserving of love and healing.

Embracing vulnerability is about dismantling the barriers we've built around our hearts. It requires courage to confront painful truths and show up fully despite fearing judgment or rejection. Sharing our stories with trusted friends or therapists can be incredibly liberating, helping us feel less isolated. As we learn to embrace our imperfections and vulnerabilities, we pave the way for deeper, more meaningful relationships.

Identifying and Processing Childhood Memories

Exploring childhood memories can be a transformative experience. It is helpful to surround yourself in a safe and supportive space where you feel comfortable reflecting on your past. One technique is to set aside quiet time each day for introspection, allowing yourself to gently revisit significant moments from your early years. Creating a timeline of your life can also be effective. Start with the earliest memories and work your way forward, noting any noteworthy events or experiences. This practice helps identify patterns and significant milestones that may need further exploration.

Another approach is guided imagery, where you visualize returning to your childhood home or favorite places from your youth. This exercise can help reconnect with forgotten memories and emotions tied to those places. Staying patient and compassionate with yourself is crucial when engaging in these techniques. Memories may not come flooding back immediately, and some might bring up feelings of discomfort or pain. Acknowledging these emotions without judgment is crucial for healing.

Seeking help from a friend, therapist, or support group can also aid this process. Sharing memories and hearing others' experiences can provide new perspectives and insights. During this exploration, professional guidance can offer structured methods and coping strategies to manage difficult emotions.

Setting aside time for journaling in your daily routine allows for uninterrupted reflection. Journaling prompts can serve as a guide when it's hard to know where to start. Prompts like "Describe a happy memory from your childhood" or "What did you fear most as a child?" encourage deep contemplation of positive and negative experiences. Through writing, you process emotions and gain clarity about past events.

Some prompts can focus on relationships, such as "Write about your relationship with your parents" or "Describe a moment when you felt misunderstood by family members." These questions help uncover the roots of current relationship patterns. Other prompts might center on specific incidents, like "Recall a time you felt incredibly proud or ashamed" or "Describe a significant loss you experienced as a child." Each prompt peels back layers of your subconscious, revealing long-buried memories and associated emotions.

Journaling consistently about your childhood experiences enables you to see growth over time. It helps you connect the dots between past and present behaviors, fostering self-awareness and providing a sense of continuity. Combining journaling with other therapeutic practices enhances healing, making it a holistic approach to inner child work.

Family dynamics play a pivotal role in shaping who we become as adults. Understanding these dynamics involves examining each family member's roles during childhood. Reflecting on how these roles influenced your behavior and interactions can shed light on deeply ingrained patterns. For instance, were you the peacemaker, the achiever, or the caretaker in your family? Recognizing these roles helps you understand the expectations and pressures placed upon you from an early age.

Analyzing family dynamics also involves looking at communication patterns. Consider how conflicts were handled in your household. Were they avoided, explosively confronted, or resolved through open dialogue? Identifying these patterns can explain how you manage conflicts as an adult. Additionally, exploring the emotional climate of your family—whether it was nurturing, critical, or neglectful—provides insights into your emotional responses and coping mechanisms.

Understanding family dynamics isn't just about blame; it's about gaining clarity and compassion. Recognizing that every family member, including yourself, has been shaped by their own experiences helps develop empathy. This understanding creates space for healing and transforming old patterns into healthier ways of relating.

Trauma recognition is a fundamental step in inner child healing. Childhood trauma can manifest in various forms—neglect, abuse, loss, or even chronic stress from living in an unstable environment. Identifying these traumas involves paying attention to triggers that activate intense emotional reactions. These could be situations, places, or even specific words that remind you of past traumatic experiences. Recognizing these triggers is the beginning step toward processing and healing them.

Working through trauma often requires professional support. A therapist trained in trauma-informed care can help navigate the complex emotions and memories that resurface. Therapies involving EMDR (Eye Movement Desensitization and Reprocessing) or somatic experiencing can be particularly effective for trauma healing. These approaches work by helping you process traumatic memories in a safe and controlled manner, lessening their impact on your present life.

Developing self-compassion is crucial in trauma recognition. It's common to feel shame or guilt about past experiences, but understanding that your responses were survival mechanisms can alleviate these feelings. Offering kindness to your inner child, who endured these hardships, is a powerful act of healing. Practicing mindfulness and grounding exercises helps you stay connected to the present moment, preventing you from being overwhelmed by past memories.

Practical Techniques and Tools for Inner Child Healing

Having self-soothing techniques at your disposal during distress can be beneficial. One effective strategy is creating a comforting environment that speaks to your inner child. This might involve surrounding yourself with items that evoke a sense of safety and warmth, such as soft blankets, stuffed animals, or favorite childhood books. Doing so creates a sanctuary where your inner child can feel secure and nurtured.

Another proper self-soothing technique is engaging in gentle physical activities, such as taking a warm bath, practicing yoga, or engaging in your particular interest. These pastimes can help release tension and promote relaxation, offering solace to your inner child. Additionally, incorporating soothing sensory experiences like listening to calming music, watching a comfort show, or drinking a warm beverage can further enhance well-being.

Developing a self-compassionate dialogue is also crucial for soothing your inner child. Speak to yourself with kindness and reassurance, like you would comfort a dear friend or child. Remind yourself that it's okay to feel vulnerable and that you're deserving of love and care. Establishing this compassionate inner dialogue can significantly alleviate distress and foster deep self-acceptance and understanding.

Grounding exercises are extraordinary tools for anchoring yourself in the present moment and alleviating anxiety. One simple grounding practice involves focusing on your breath. Take slow, deep breaths, paying close attention to the sensation of air entering and leaving your body. This mindful breathing can help shift your focus from anxious thoughts and usher you back to the here and now.

Engaging your senses through grounding techniques can provide immediate relief from anxiety. For example, you could use the 5-4-3-2-1 method to identify five things you can see, four things you can touch, three things you can hear, two things you can smell, and one thing you can taste. This exercise helps to interrupt anxious thought patterns and fosters a sense of connection to your surroundings.

Physical grounding can also be practical, such as pressing your feet firmly into the ground or holding onto a solid object. These actions create a tangible connection to the present moment, helping to stabilize your emotions and reduce overwhelming feelings. Regular grounding exercises can build resilience and enhance your ability to manage anxiety over time.

Cultivating self-compassion is essential for nurturing your inner child. One way to practice self-compassion is with mindfulness meditation. This exercise encourages you to observe your thoughts and feelings without judgment, allowing you to embrace your inner child's experiences with empathy and understanding.

Inner child healing can be a powerful technique for late-diagnosed autistic adults, helping to address past traumas and foster self-acceptance. Here is a method specifically designed for inner child healing:

Inner Child Healing Technique: Compassionate Dialogue

Purpose:

This technique aims to reconnect with and nurture your inner child, fostering self-compassion and healing past wounds.

Steps:

1. **Create a Safe Space** :

   - Find a quiet, comfortable spot where you won't be disturbed. This could be a cozy corner of your home or a peaceful place in nature.

3. **Relax and Center Yourself** :

   - Sit or lie down comfortably. Close your eyes and take a few slow breaths, drawing in through your nose and exhaling through your mouth. Allow your body to relax with each breath.

5. **Visualize Your Inner Child** :

   - Imagine a younger version of yourself. This could be at any age when you felt particularly vulnerable or needed support. Picture this younger self in as much detail as possible.

7. **Initiate a Dialogue** :

   - Begin a compassionate dialogue with your inner child. You can do this silently in your mind or by speaking softly out loud. Start with a gentle greeting, like:

     - "Hello, little [Your Name]. I see you, and I'm here to listen."

9. **Listen to Your Inner Child's Needs** :

   ○ Ask your inner child how they are feeling and what they need. For example:

     ▪ "How are you feeling right now?"

     ▪ "What do you need to feel safe and loved?"

   ○ Permit your inner child to reveal their feelings and needs without judgment. Listen and acknowledge their emotions.

11. **Offer Comfort and Reassurance** :

   ○ Provide comfort and reassurance to your inner child. Speak to them as you would to a beloved child or friend. Examples include:

     ▪ "It's okay to feel scared. I'm here with you, and you're safe."

     ▪ "You are loved just as you are. You don't have to be anything different."

13. **Validate Their Experience** :

   ○ Validate your inner child's experiences and emotions. Let them know that their feelings are real and vital. For example:

     ▪ "It's okay to feel hurt about what happened. Your feelings are valid."

     ▪ "You have every right to feel the way you do. It's okay to feel sad or angry."

15. **Visualize Nurturing Activities** :

   ○ Imagine engaging in nurturing activities with your inner child. This could be soothing and comforting, like hugging, playing, or reading a story together. Visualize providing the love and care your inner child needs.

17. **Express Love and Acceptance** :

   - End the dialogue by expressing love and acceptance. Reassure your inner child that they are always welcome and that you will continue to be there for them. Examples include:

     - "I love you and will always be here for you."

     - "You are perfect, just as you are, and I am proud of you."

19. **Return to the Present** :

   - Gradually guide your conciousness back to the present moment. Take a few slow breaths and gently open your eyes. Please take a moment to reflect on the experience and how it made you feel.

Example Dialogue in Practice:

1. **Greeting** :

   - "Hello, little [Your Name]. I see you, and I'm here to listen."

3. **Listening** :

   - "How are you feeling right now?"

   - Inner Child: "I feel scared and alone."

   - "It's okay to feel scared. I'm here with you, and you're safe. What do you need to feel better?"

5. **Offering Comfort** :

   - "You are loved just as you are. You don't have to be anything different."

7. **Validating** :
   - "It's okay to feel hurt about what happened. Your feelings are valid."

9. **Nurturing Activity** :
   - "Let's imagine we're sitting under a big tree, reading your favorite story together. You are safe and loved."

11. **Expressing Love** :
   - "I love you and will always be here for you."

Benefits:

- **Fosters Self-Compassion** : Encourages a kind and compassionate relationship with oneself.
- **Heals Past Wounds** : Helps to address and heal past traumas and emotional wounds.
- **Promotes Self-Acceptance** : Enhances self-acceptance and love for one's true self.
- **Reduces Anxiety and Stress** : Provides a calming and comforting experience, reducing overall anxiety and stress.

Regularly practicing this inner child healing technique can nurture your emotional well-being and cultivate a more compassionate and accepting relationship with yourself.

Another self-compassion practice involves writing a compassionate letter to yourself. In this letter, acknowledge your struggles, offer encouragement, and express forgiveness for any perceived shortcomings. This act of self-kindness can be profoundly healing, reinforcing your inner child's sense of worth and belonging.

Incorporating self-compassion breaks into your daily routine can also be beneficial. During these breaks, take a moment to acknowledge any discomfort or pain you're experiencing, then respond with gentle reassurance and care. Remember that imperfection is part of the human experience, and grant yourself the same grace and compassion you would offer to a loved one. Regularly practicing self-compassion can transform your relationship with your inner child, fostering a deep sense of peace and acceptance (Self-compassion practices. Self-Compassion., n.d).

Mindfulness and breathing practices are essential for connecting with your inner child and promoting inner peace. Start with simple mindfulness practices, such as focusing on the present moment and recognizing your thoughts and feelings without judgment. This awareness can help you better understand and address your inner child's needs.

Guided visualizations can also be an effective way to connect with your inner child. Picture yourself meeting your inner child in a safe and loving environment where you can offer comfort and support. Visualize giving your inner child a hug or sitting together peacefully, reinforcing a sense of security and love.

Successful Inner Child Healing Journeys

My Healing Journey offers a profound insight into reconnecting with one's inner child and overcoming past trauma. My story begins in my mid-forties when I, for the first time, sought professional help to address lingering feelings of inadequacy and persistent anxiety. Diagnosed late in life with ADHD and autism, I realized that many of my struggles could be traced back to unprocessed childhood experiences and trauma. By looking into these recollections with the guidance of my therapist, I embarked on a path toward healing that would ultimately transform my self-perception and quality of life.

Reflecting on my childhood, I uncovered significant moments that shaped my adult identity. As a young girl, my peers and teachers often misunderstood me and frequently admonished me for being "too quiet" or "daydreaming." These incidents gradually eroded my self-esteem, leading me to develop coping mechanisms centered around masking my true nature to fit societal expectations. Through guided reflection exercises, I pinpointed how these early experiences influenced my relationships and work habits, shedding light on patterns I had considered intrinsic aspects of my personality. This newfound clarity allowed me to understand my behaviors not as personal failings but as responses to my environment, setting the stage for more profound healing.

Integral to my journey were the therapeutic interventions employed by my therapist. Cognitive Processing Therapy (CPT) played a pivotal role, helping to reframe negative beliefs about myself derived from my traumatic experiences. In tandem, Inner Child Work enabled me to visualize and interact with my younger self, creating a nurturing space for us both. Techniques like guided imagery and narrative therapy facilitated dialogue between me and my inner child, fostering a compassionate relationship where I learned to offer love and acceptance to parts of myself previously riddled with shame and guilt. These methods were instrumental in breaking down long-held barriers to emotional intimacy and self-acceptance.

As I continued my inner child healing work, I experienced remarkable transformation and growth. I began to embrace my authentic self, acknowledging my unique strengths and needs without the mask I had worn for so long. This shift was evident in various aspects of my life - I discovered a new level of creativity, set healthier boundaries in relationships, and experienced a substantial reduction in anxiety. I also became more attuned to my needs, practicing self-care and utilizing coping strategies that honored my individuality. The healing journey is neither quick nor linear, but it was profoundly liberating, allowing me to move forward with a sense of wholeness and empowerment. I remain on my path of unmasking and will forever.

Readers will gain insight into the cathartic power of inner child work, understanding how embracing vulnerability and reconnecting with their past can lead to profound healing and self-acceptance.

Throughout this chapter, we've delved into the intricate process of inner child healing, focusing on its significance for late-diagnosed autistic adults and individuals with ADHD. We've explored how reconnecting with our inner child can unlock hidden emotions, resolve past conflicts, and lead to profound self-discovery.

We began by identifying the lingering presence of our inner child and understanding how childhood experiences shape our current selves. Recognizing these connections gives us valuable insights into our behaviors, emotional responses, and self-perceptions. The journey involves acknowledging and nurturing your inner child through therapeutic practices like guided visualization and writing letters, fostering a sense of integration and wholeness.

A significant part of this work involves embracing vulnerability. Protective mechanisms developed in childhood can hinder our ability to be open and authentic as adults. However, embracing vulnerability is a powerful pathway to inner strength and resilience. It allows us to heal old wounds, build genuine connections, and foster more profound self-acceptance.

Reflecting on specific childhood memories uncovers patterns that explain present-day behaviors. This process of exploration requires patience and persistence. Engaging in beloved activities from childhood or seeking therapy and support groups can provide additional guidance and encouragement. Creating a safe internal environment where your inner child feels seen and heard is crucial. Techniques like mindfulness meditation aid in listening to your inner child's needs, reinforcing that you are capable and deserving of love and healing.

Another critical aspect is the emphasis on addressing trauma and family dynamics. Recognizing early roles and communication patterns within our families helps us understand deeply ingrained behaviors. Trauma recognition, supported by professional guidance, is essential. Eye

Movement Desensitization and Reprocessing (EMDR) is a psychotherapy technique designed to reduce the distress associated with traumatic memories. Engaging in bilateral stimulation provided in EMDR therapy (eye movements, taps, or sounds) is believed to aid in processing and integrating traumatic memories. This may reduce the emotional intensity associated with these memories, improving overall emotional well-being. This process is akin to how the brain processes information during REM sleep. Developing self-compassion is crucial in this context, as it enables us to show kindness to our inner child who has experienced hardships.

We've also discussed practical techniques and tools for connecting with your inner child. Self-soothing strategies, grounding exercises, and self-compassion practices create a nurturing environment for your inner child. These methods promote relaxation, alleviate anxiety, and foster a deep sense of self-acceptance. Mindfulness and breathing exercises enhance this connection, helping you better understand and address your inner child's needs.

My healing journey illustrates that reconnecting with one's inner child can lead to remarkable transformation and growth. By understanding and addressing my past, I am embracing my authentic self, setting healthier boundaries, and reducing anxiety. My experience underscores the liberating power of inner child healing, paving the way for a sense of wholeness and empowerment. It remains an ongoing endeavor that I persistently dedicate myself to improving.

In conclusion, inner child healing offers a transformative path toward unmasking and self-discovery for late-diagnosed autistic adults and individuals with ADHD. While the journey may be challenging, embracing authenticity and fostering self-acceptance is an opportunity. As you continue this process, remember to be patient and compassionate with yourself. By nurturing your inner child, you're taking vital steps toward a more integrated and fulfilling life. What awaits beyond this healing journey is a deeper understanding of yourself and a newfound sense of freedom and peace.

Embracing Neurodiversity: Celebrating Differences

E mbracing neurodiversity means appreciating how individuals with different neurological conditions think, learn, and interact with the world. The term "neurodiversity" emphasizes that there are many ways of experiencing life, and none is superior to another. By understanding this concept, we can recognize the intrinsic value in the diversity of human minds. Neurodiversity is about acknowledging and celebrating differences as an integral part of our social fabric. It challenges traditional perspectives that often pathologize neurological differences, creating a more inclusive society where everyone feels valued.

This chapter will explore various facets of neurodiversity, including its societal implications and the strengths that neurodivergent individuals bring to different aspects of life. We will discuss the importance of moving beyond deficit-focused views and the necessity of implementing inclusive practices in educational and professional settings. By fostering empathy and understanding, we aim to create a society that accommodates and celebrates neurological differences. This chapter will examine how embracing neurodiversity benefits everyone, leading to more innovative solutions, richer communities, and a more compassionate world.

Discussing the Concept of Neurodiversity and Its Societal Implications

Understanding neurodiversity is a fundamental aspect of embracing diversity within the neurodiverse community. "Neurodiversity" refers to the variety in human brain function and behavioral traits. It highlights that no single way of thinking, learning, or behaving is superior; all variations are valuable. This concept emerged in the 1990s and has since gained momentum, advocating for the acceptance and inclusion of people with neurological differences such as autism, ADHD, and dyslexia. By understanding neurodiversity, we can appreciate the vast array of perspectives and abilities that enrich our world (Baumer et al., 2021).

Acknowledging the spectrum of neurodivergent traits and strengths in individuals is crucial. Every individual within the neurodiverse community possesses a unique combination of abilities and challenges. For instance, someone with autism may have exceptionally high concentration levels and innovative thinking. At the same time, another may excel in problem-solving approaches and have a deep empathy for causes, leading to powerful advocacy. Recognizing these strengths allows us to move beyond a deficit-focused view and instead see neurodivergent individuals as societal contributors. This acknowledgment fosters a more inclusive environment where diverse skills are celebrated and utilized effectively.

Challenging traditional views of neurodiversity as a deficit is necessary for shifting societal perspectives. Historically, neurological differences have often been pathologized, seen as conditions to be fixed or cured. This perspective perpetuates stigma and exclusion. However, by reframing neurodiversity as a natural variation, we can challenge these outdated notions. Embracing neurodiversity means recognizing that differences are not inherently harmful but rather part of the rich tapestry of human experience. This shift in mindset is critical for creating a more accepting and supportive society.

Promoting acceptance and accommodation for diverse neurological structures is essential. Inclusive practices must be implemented in various settings such as schools, workplaces, and communities. For example, providing flexible work hours, sensory-friendly spaces, and clear communication guidelines can significantly enhance the experiences of neurodivergent individuals. These accommodations support their unique needs and promote their strengths and contributions. Creating an environment that values and adapts to diverse neurological structures ensures that everyone has the opportunity to thrive.

The social implications of neurodiversity are profound, impacting society on multiple levels. When we embrace neurodiversity, we open doors to a more inclusive and equitable community. This acceptance reduces stigma and discrimination, allowing neurodivergent individuals to participate in all respects in social, educational, and professional settings. Also, fostering an inclusive culture can lead to innovative solutions and ideas, as diverse perspectives bring new insights and approaches to problem-solving.

Embracing neurodiversity benefits individuals and society by promoting creativity, empathy, and collaboration.

Encouraging empathy and understanding towards individuals with different cognitive perspectives is vital for fostering inclusivity. Empathy allows us to put ourselves in others' shoes, appreciating their unique experiences and challenges. By educating ourselves about neurodiversity and actively listening to neurodivergent voices, we can build stronger connections and create a more compassionate community. Understanding that everyone's brain works differently helps to break down barriers and promotes mutual respect. This empathetic approach is critical to supporting neurodivergent individuals daily and ensuring they feel valued and understood.

Advocating for policies and methods that support neurodiverse individuals in education, employment, and other societal aspects is necessary for systemic change. Policies that mandate reasonable accommodations and anti-discrimination measures help create environments where neurodivergent individuals can succeed. Educational programs that incorporate neurodiversity awareness can equip teachers and students with the knowledge to support diverse learners effectively. In the workplace, inclusive hiring practices and professional development opportunities ensure that neurodivergent employees can contribute and advance their careers. Systemic support through policies and practices is crucial for achieving long-term equity and inclusion for neurodiverse individuals.

Creating space for authentic self-expression and valuing diverse contributions allows neurodivergent individuals to thrive. Authentic self-expression means that neurodivergent people can be themselves without masking their differences. It involves celebrating their unique ways of thinking, learning, and interacting with the world. Valuing diverse contributions means recognizing and utilizing the strengths that neurodivergent individuals exhibit. When neurodivergent individuals feel accepted and valued, they are more likely to contribute positively and meaningfully to their communities and workplaces.

Understanding neurodiversity is a fundamental aspect of embracing diversity within the neurodiverse community. "Neurodiversity" refers to the variety in human brain function and behavioral traits. It highlights that no single way of thinking, learning, or behaving is superior; all variations are valuable. This concept has since gained momentum, advocating for the acceptance and involvement of people with neurological differences such as autism, ADHD, and dyslexia. By understanding neurodiversity, we can appreciate the vast array of perspectives and abilities that enrich our world (DCEG, 2022).

Acknowledging the spectrum of neurodivergent traits and strengths in individuals is crucial. Every individual within the neurodiverse community possesses a unique combination of abilities and challenges. Recognizing these strengths allows us to move beyond a deficit-focused view and instead see neurodivergent individuals as societal contributors. This acknowledgment fosters a more inclusive environment where diverse skills are celebrated and utilized effectively.

Exploring Ways to Celebrate and Advocate for Neurodiverse Communities

Engaging with neurodiverse communities to foster a sense of belonging is essential. This engagement starts with active participation and creating spaces where neurodiverse individuals feel valued and understood. Community centers, support groups, and online forums can offer safe environments for sharing experiences and building connections. These platforms help neurodiverse individuals realize they are not alone and that their differences are strengths rather than shortcomings.

Another crucial aspect of community engagement involves promoting mutual support. When people come together, they can share resources, advocate for each other, and provide emotional support during challenging times. Encouraging mentorship programs where experienced members guide newcomers can create a robust support network. This inclusivity fosters resilience and empowers neurodiverse individuals to navigate their unique challenges confidently.

Lastly, fostering a sense of belonging involves wholeheartedly listening to the needs and desires of the neurodiverse community. Hosting regular community meetings and feedback sessions ensures that everyone's voice is heard. We can tailor initiatives to better serve the community by implementing their suggestions. This collaborative approach demonstrates respect and appreciation for neurodiverse perspectives, creating a more inclusive and supportive environment.

Participating in neurodiversity events, forums, and advocacy groups is another vital way to celebrate and advocate for neurodiverse communities. These gatherings offer opportunities for neurodiverse individuals to connect, share stories, and promote understanding. Events like Neurodiversity Awareness Week or specialized conferences create public platforms for discussing essential issues and celebrating diversity.

Forums and advocacy groups extend these opportunities by providing ongoing support and education. Online forums allow continuous communication, while advocacy groups work towards systemic change. They engage in campaigns to raise awareness, influence policy, and ensure that neurodiverse voices are represented. Joining these organizations can amplify individual efforts, making advocacy more effective and widespread.

Additionally, participating in these activities can be empowering for neurodiverse individuals themselves. It offers a chance to take an active role in molding their community and advocating for their rights. By seeing tangible results from their involvement, such as changes in legislation or increased public awareness, individuals can achieve a sense of success and purpose, further reinforcing their self-worth and contribution to society.

Supporting legislative efforts for neurodiversity inclusion and accessibility is critical. Legislators need to hear from neurodiverse individuals and advocates about the barriers they face and the changes required. Supporting laws that mandate accessible workplaces, schools, and public spaces ensures everyone has the opportunity to thrive. Advocacy can involve meeting with policymakers, testifying at hearings, and rallying public support for these initiatives.

Raising lawmakers' awareness of the importance of neurodiversity is an ongoing process. Educating them about the benefits of diverse perspectives can lead to more complete and inclusive policies. This can include presenting data, personal stories, and successful case studies from other regions or countries that have embraced neurodiversity and seen positive outcomes.

Finally, supporting legislative efforts also means holding policymakers accountable. Regular follow-ups and publicizing their commitments can keep the momentum going. Empowering neurodiverse individuals to participate in this advocacy ensures that those directly affected by the policies have a say in shaping them. This level of involvement is crucial for achieving lasting and meaningful change.

Empowering neurodiverse individuals to advocate for themselves and their community is fundamental to creating lasting change. Self-advocacy begins with education and awareness. Providing neurodiverse people with information about their rights and available resources equips them with the tools necessary for effective advocacy. Workshops, training programs, and accessible informational materials can help build these skills.

Another way to empower individuals is to create opportunities for leadership within the neurodiverse community. Encouraging neurodiverse people to take on roles within organizations, community groups, or advocacy initiatives allows them to lead by example. Seeing peers in leadership positions can inspire others to take charge of their advocacy journey, fostering a culture of empowerment and mutual support.

Moreover, it's essential to provide platforms where neurodiverse individuals can share their experiences and insights. Public speaking engagements, writing opportunities, and social media campaigns give neurodiverse voices a wider audience. Highlighting personal stories and achievements celebrates diversity and challenges stereotypes, helping shift societal perceptions toward greater acceptance and inclusion.

Providing Educational Tools for Spreading Awareness About Neurodiversity

Educational outreach plays a vital role in promoting neurodiversity awareness. Developing robust training programs for schools, workplaces, and communities can significantly enhance the understanding and acceptance of neurodiverse individuals. These training programs should be designed with input from neurodivergent individuals to ensure they address real-world challenges and foster empathy. In schools, such programs can help students appreciate the diverse ways their peers learn and interact with the world. In workplaces, they can create more inclusive environments where neurodiverse employees feel valued and understood. Community training programs can educate the general public, making everyday interactions more compassionate and supportive for neurodiverse individuals.

In these training programs, it is essential to include practical strategies that participants can implement daily. For example, schools can incorporate flexible teaching methods and provide sensory-friendly spaces. Workplaces can offer accommodations like quiet workspaces or flexible schedules. Community programs can teach people to communicate effectively with neurodiverse individuals, recognizing and respecting their unique needs. By equipping people with concrete tools and knowledge, these training programs can significantly impact the lives of neurodiverse individuals and foster a more inclusive society.

Leveraging various platforms and methods can be beneficial. Online courses, workshops, and webinars can make the information accessible to a broader audience. Collaborating with local organizations and advocacy groups can also help spread awareness and ensure the training programs are relevant and impactful. Continuous feedback from neurodiverse individuals and experts can help refine and improve the programs, making them more effective and responsive to the needs of the neurodiverse community.

Creating informational materials such as brochures, videos, and presentations is another effective way to raise awareness about neurodiversity. These materials should be easily understandable and visually engaging to capture the attention of a broad audience. Brochures can be distributed in schools, workplaces, community centers, and healthcare facilities, providing concise and valuable information about neurodiversity. Videos and presentations can be shared online and used in training sessions, offering deeper insights and personal stories to illustrate the importance of embracing neurodiversity.

When designing these informational materials, it's crucial to highlight the strengths and contributions of neurodiverse individuals. Sharing success stories and positive experiences can challenge stereotypes and shift perceptions from viewing neurodiversity as a deficit to recognizing it as a valuable aspect of human diversity. Including quotes and testimonials from neurodiverse individuals can add authenticity and resonate with a broader audience. Visual aids, infographics, and interactive elements can make the information more appealing and easier to understand, catering to different learning styles.

Collaborating with professionals such as graphic designers, educators, and neurodiversity advocates can enhance the quality and effectiveness of these materials. Regularly updating and expanding the content ensures it remains relevant and aligned with the latest research and societal trends. By distributing these materials widely and making them accessible, we can foster greater awareness and appreciation for neurodiversity, ultimately contributing to a more inclusive and accepting society.

Another crucial educational outreach aspect is collaborating with educators and experts to integrate neurodiversity topics into curricula. This ensures that future generations grow up with a better understanding and acceptance of neurodiverse individuals. Schools play an essential role in forming young minds, and incorporating neurodiversity education can help children develop empathy and respect for their neurodiverse peers. Curricula can include lessons on different learning styles, sensory processing issues, and the strengths associated with neurodiverse conditions.

Working closely with teachers and educational institutions is essential to tailor the curricula to fit different age groups and learning environments. Professional development for teachers can provide them with the skills and knowledge to support neurodiverse students effectively. Expert input can ensure that the information presented is accurate and comprehensive. Including neurodiverse voices in the development process can provide valuable insights and ensure that the curricula genuinely reflect the experiences and needs of neurodiverse individuals (Awareness and Education. Stanford Neurodiversity Project., n.d.).

Integrating neurodiversity topics into curricula can also involve creating projects and activities encouraging students to explore and celebrate differences. For instance, students can collaborate on projects that highlight the unique talents and perspectives of their neurodiverse classmates. These tasks can encourage a sense of community and reinforce the message that diversity is a strength. By embedding neurodiversity education into the core of the curriculum, we can nurture a generation that values and respects all forms of diversity (Neurodiversity Hub - Resources for Students, Employers & More. Neurodiversity Hub., n.d.).

Media representation plays a consequential role in shaping societal perceptions of neurodiversity. Accurate and positive portrayals of neurodiverse characters in films, television shows, books, and other media can help break down stereotypes and promote inclusivity. Media creators must consult with neurodiverse individuals and experts to ensure authenticity in their representation. Depicting neurodiverse characters in various roles and narratives helps normalize neurodiversity and demonstrates that neurodiverse individuals can lead fulfilling and successful lives like anyone else.

Analyzing media stereotypes and promoting authentic representation of neurodivergent traits is crucial in this endeavor. Often, neurodiverse characters are portrayed in a one-dimensional manner, either as savants or as individuals who are solely defined by their condition. Such representations can perpetuate misconceptions and fail to capture the richness and complexity of neurodiverse lives. Encouraging media creators to portray neurodiverse characters with depth and nuance can help audiences develop a more accurate and empathetic understanding of neurodiversity.

Collaborating with neurodiverse writers, actors, and consultants can significantly enhance the authenticity of media portrayals. Their lived experiences can inform storylines and character development, ensuring that neurodiverse characters are represented with dignity and respect. Supporting media outlets that feature diverse and inclusive narratives can also drive demand for better representation. By challenging stereotypes and advocating for genuine portrayals, we can use media as a powerful device to promote neurodiversity awareness and acceptance.

Encouraging media outlets to feature neurodiverse individuals in diverse roles and narratives goes beyond fictional portrayals. Documentaries, interviews, and reality shows that highlight the achievements and everyday lives of neurodiverse individuals can provide valuable insights and humanize their experiences. Featuring neurodiverse individuals in various fields, from science to arts to sports, can showcase their contributions and inspire others. Media partnerships and campaigns focused on neurodiversity can amplify these efforts and lead to broader discussion.

Supporting neurodiversity awareness campaigns through media partnerships can further enhance visibility and impact. These campaigns can leverage the power of social media, television, radio, and print to spread messages of acceptance and inclusion. Collaborating with influencers and celebrities who advocate for neurodiversity can attract more attention and engagement. Public service announcements, special features, and dedicated segments on popular shows can keep the conversation going and maintain public interest in neurodiversity issues.

Sharing Personal Stories Highlighting the Beauty of Neurodiversity

Personal stories are powerful tools for understanding the beauty of neurodiversity. They offer glimpses into the lives of neurodiverse individuals, revealing a spectrum of experiences that shape their unique perspectives. One such example is Lisa, a young woman diagnosed with autism in her early twenties. Lisa found that her hyperfocus, initially seen as a drawback in traditional educational settings, allowed her to excel in intricate art forms. Her detailed sculptures symbolized patience and precision, challenging the stereotype that autism limits creativity.

These narratives are windows into worlds often misunderstood or unseen. Another inspiring story comes from Jack, who was diagnosed with ADHD at a young age. The school was a struggle for him due to the constant need to move and his difficulty focusing on tasks for extended periods. However, he thrived once he discovered his passion for sports, particularly basketball. His boundless energy, problematic in a classroom, became his greatest asset on the court. Jack's story showcases how environments that align with individual strengths can unlock potential previously overshadowed by perceived weaknesses.

Diverse experiences within the neurodiverse community demonstrate the array of talents and abilities these individuals bring to the table. Take, for instance, Maria, a software developer with dyslexia. Traditional reading methods were challenging, but she developed innovative strategies to comprehend complex texts and codes. Her unique approach caught the attention of her peers, leading to her becoming a mentor for others with similar challenges. Maria's journey emphasizes recognizing and nurturing different learning styles, benefiting individuals and the broader community.

Sharing stories of resilience, creativity, and unique strengths exhibited by neurodiverse individuals enriches our understanding of human potential. One compelling example is Sam, an autistic teenager who struggled with social interactions but excelled in music. Through relentless practice and a deep connection with his instrument, Sam could communicate emotions and stories that he found hard to express verbally. His performances captivated audiences, illustrating that neurodiversity can profoundly enhance artistic expression.

The resilience of neurodiverse individuals is also evident in the story of Emma, who has ADHD. Despite being told she would never succeed academically, Emma pursued a degree in engineering. She implemented personalized techniques for managing her time and staying organized, transforming her learning approach. Today, Emma leads a successful career in aerospace engineering, where her innovative thinking and problem-solving skills are highly valued. Her story highlights the significance of perseverance and adaptation in overcoming obstacles and achieving success.

Creativity blossoms in neurodiverse minds, as seen in the case of Mark, a dyslexic writer who struggled with conventional literacy throughout school. Instead of viewing his dyslexia as a barrier, Mark turned to spoken word poetry, where he could harness his vivid imagination and solid auditory skills. His performances address societal issues and captivate audiences worldwide. Mark's journey highlights how embracing alternative modes of communication can lead to groundbreaking contributions to the arts.

Neurodiversity holds immense value in enriching communities and driving innovation. Consider the tech industry, where neurodiverse individuals often excel. For instance, Clara, who has autism, is a data analyst. Her ability to recognize patterns and focus intensely on tasks makes her exceptionally good at identifying trends others might overlook. Clara's contributions have led to significant advancements in her company's data processing capabilities, showcasing how neurodiverse talent can drive progress in technology and other fields.

In another example, Alex, who has ADHD, founded a startup specializing in eco-friendly packaging solutions. His restless energy and rapid idea generation, often seen as disruptive in school, catalyzed innovation in his business. By leveraging his strengths, Alex developed products that garnered commercial success and contributed positively to environmental sustainability. These stories affirm that when neurodiverse individuals are given opportunities to thrive, they can effect meaningful change and innovation within society.

Communities become more dynamic when they embrace neurodiversity. Take Zoe, a community leader with dyslexia who champions inclusive education. Her advocacy work ensures that educational systems accommodate different learning needs, ensuring no child is left behind. Zoe's initiatives have created a more supportive and inclusive environment for all students, highlighting the pivotal role neurodiverse individuals play in fostering equitable societies.

Amplifying the voices of neurodiverse individuals is essential to challenging stereotypes and promoting acceptance. One way this can be achieved is through public speaking engagements, like those organized by colleges catering to neurodivergent students. At Landmark College, for instance, students share their personal stories during commencement speeches. These narratives, filled with triumphs and tribulations, resonate deeply with audiences and help dismantle preconceived notions about neurodiversity (Shmulsky, S., 2022).

Furthermore, media representation plays a critical role in shaping perceptions. Films, books, and TV shows featuring authentically portrayed neurodiverse characters can foster empathy and understanding. As seen with popular series that include characters with autism or ADHD, accurate depiction helps normalize neurodiversity, making it part of everyday discourse. This, in turn, encourages a more accepting and supportive society.

Storytelling also takes the form of written narratives. Autobiographies and memoirs by neurodiverse authors provide firsthand insights into their experiences. These literary works serve as noteworthy tools for educating the public and advocating for the rights and inclusion of neurodiverse individuals. Encouraging neurodiverse voices in literature can break down barriers and promote a broader understanding of what it means to live with a neurodevelopmental condition.

Reinforcing the importance of embracing differences and nurturing a culture of acceptance.

This chapter has explored the profound concept of neurodiversity and its implications for society. By understanding neurodiversity as the natural variation in human brain function and behavioral traits, we appreciate that no single way of thinking or learning is superior. This recognition lays the foundation for a more inclusive and accepting community that values the unique strengths and perspectives of neurodiverse individuals.

Reflecting on the introduction, where we began our journey into the world of neurodiversity, it is apparent how critical it is to acknowledge and celebrate these differences. Every individual within the neurodiverse community carries a distinct blend of abilities and challenges. Recognizing these strengths allows us to move past a deficit-based viewpoint and see neurodivergent individuals as invaluable societal contributors. This shift in perspective fosters an environment where diverse skills are celebrated and utilized effectively.

Currently, our stance is clear: embracing neurodiversity is essential. Promoting acceptance and accommodation for varied neurological profiles requires proactive efforts across all societal settings. Schools, workplaces, and communities must implement inclusive practices such as flexible schedules, sensory-friendly environments, and clear communication guidelines. These changes not only support neurodivergent individuals by meeting their needs but also enhance their contributions, ensuring everyone can thrive.

Some readers might be concerned about the challenges of creating such an inclusive society. It's crucial to remember that shifting societal perspectives and implementing accommodations can be complex and resource-intensive. However, the broader consequences of embracing neurodiversity are immensely positive. We open doors to innovative solutions and ideas by creating an environment that values all individuals, regardless of their neurological makeup. Diverse perspectives enrich problem-solving processes, leading to groundbreaking advancements in various fields.

Promoting neurodiversity has significant social implications on a broader scale. It reduces stigma and discrimination, allowing neurodivergent individuals to participate wholly in social, educational, and professional contexts. An inclusive society benefits neurodivergent individuals; it enhances the collective creativity, empathy, and collaboration of the entire community. By constructing a culture of respect and understanding, we pave the way for a brighter, more equitable future.

In conclusion, embracing neurodiversity is ongoing and requires continuous effort and dedication. As we move forward, let us remain committed to creating spaces where neurodivergent individuals can express themselves authentically and feel valued for their unique contributions. We contribute to a more harmonious world by fostering inclusivity and celebrating diversity. The question now is, how will each of us take part in this important endeavor?

The Role of Therapy: Professional Guidance on the Journey

T he role of therapy in the journey of unmasking and healing for late-diagnosed individuals with autism and ADHD is profound. Navigating the complexities of these neurodiverse conditions requires more than self-reflection; it necessitates professional guidance to uncover deep-seated behaviors and develop effective coping strategies. Therapy allows for a structured environment where individuals can investigate their authentic selves with the support of an experienced professional who understands their unique challenges.

In this chapter, we will sift through the intricacies of finding the right therapist, ensuring their expertise aligns with the specific needs of late-diagnosed adults. We will also explore how personalized therapy approaches can foster a sense of validation and support, making the therapeutic journey more compelling. Furthermore, the chapter will cover various therapeutic methodologies that enhance the unmasking process, focusing on creating a personalized approach to reach each individual's needs. By examining these aspects, readers will gain valuable insights into leveraging professional guidance to navigate their paths toward authenticity and self-acceptance.

Finding the Right Therapist

Finding the right therapist who is experienced in working with late-diagnosed autism and ADHD can significantly enhance one's unmasking journey. Understanding these nuances is crucial as it allows the therapist to address specific challenges faced by individuals diagnosed later in life. This understanding enables the therapist to offer a more compassionate and informed approach, fostering an environment where the client feels understood and supported.

Late-diagnosed individuals often face unique hurdles, such as years of masking behaviors and internalized stigma. A specialist therapist recognizes these patterns and provides tailored strategies to dismantle them. By acknowledging these specific experiences, the therapist can help the client navigate their journey more easily. This personalization also helps create a therapeutic alliance based on empathy and validation.

Furthermore, selecting the right therapist involves considering their expertise and methodologies. Therapists with a deep knowledge of autism and ADHD are more likely to employ techniques that resonate with the client's lived experiences. Their approaches can adapt to the specific ways neurodiverse individuals process emotions and interactions, making therapy sessions more effective and meaningful.

Tailoring treatment approaches to individual neurodiversity is another essential aspect of effective therapy. Each person's experience with autism or ADHD is unique, necessitating a customized therapeutic approach. By recognizing and respecting this diversity, therapists can encourage a supportive environment conducive to growth and healing.

A one-size-fits-all approach rarely works in therapy, particularly for late-diagnosed adults. Personalized therapy plans consider the individual's strengths, challenges, and preferences, thus ensuring that the support provided is relevant and actionable. This customization helps clients feel seen and heard, enhancing their comfort and willingness to engage in the therapeutic process.

In addition, the therapist's flexibility in adjusting their methods according to the client's needs facilitates a more empowering therapeutic relationship. Clients feel more motivated to participate when they know their therapy is designed uniquely for them. This tailored approach not only aids in the unmasking process but also encourages self-acceptance and personal growth.

Assessing the therapist's background is vital to ensuring that they can provide tailored and practical support. This involves looking at their credentials, areas of specialization, and previous experience with neurodiverse clients. Ensuring that the therapist has adequate training in autism—and ADHD-specific interventions is imperative for receiving appropriate care.

Understanding a therapist's professional history can reveal if they have dealt with cases similar to yours. For instance, therapists who have extensive experience working with late-diagnosed adults are likely to be more adept at addressing the intricate aspects of masking and unmasking behaviors. This experience equips them with insights and tools to guide clients toward healing and self-discovery.

Moreover, verifying the therapist's qualifications reassures clients about their ability and commitment to providing quality care. It reduces apprehensions and builds confidence in the therapeutic process. Knowing that your therapist is well-versed in your needs lays a strong foundation for a productive, trusting therapeutic relationship.

Establishing trust with a skilled professional is crucial for personal growth. Trust forms the bedrock of any effective therapeutic relationship, allowing clients to open up and explore deeply rooted issues without fear of judgment. A trustworthy therapist creates a safe space where clients can be vulnerable and honest about their thoughts and feelings.

Building trust takes time and effort from each party. The therapist must demonstrate reliability, consistency, and genuine concern for the client's well-being. Therapists can earn their clients' trust and encourage reciprocal openness through active listening, empathy, and appropriate responses. This mutual trust enhances the therapeutic bond and facilitates deeper exploration and progress.

Therapeutic Approaches Beneficial for Unmasking

Therapy can play a vital role in assisting individuals in unmasking and understanding their true selves. Cognitive Behavioral Therapy (CBT) is especially supportive in this regard. CBT focuses on examining thought patterns and behaviors that may contribute to masking. By identifying negative thinking patterns and how they affect behavior, individuals can understand why they might present a sure way to the world. This newfound awareness allows for a more profound understanding of oneself and lays the groundwork for authentic living.

One primary goal of CBT is to promote self-awareness by exploring these thought patterns. For instance, a person with ADHD might have internalized the idea that being spontaneous or unpredictable is undesirable. Through CBT, they can explore these thoughts and recognize how such beliefs influence their behavior, often leading them to mask their true feelings and actions. By identifying these patterns, individuals can begin challenging and changing them, reducing the need to mask and allowing for more genuine self-expression.

Additionally, CBT provides tools to manage negative emotions effectively. Acknowledging the connection between their thoughts, feelings, and behaviors helps individuals better control their reactions. This heightened emotional regulation is vital for those who habitually mask their emotions to fit societal norms. By learning to manage and express emotions appropriately, individuals can feel more comfortable being themselves, reducing the reliance on masking behaviors.

Restructuring cognitive distortions is another critical aspect of CBT that facilitates authenticity. Cognitive distortions are irrational or exaggerated thought patterns that can create a distorted view of oneself and the world. These distortions often lead to behaviors that reinforce masking. For example, individuals might engage in black-and-white thinking, believing they must be perfect in social situations to be accepted. This belief can drive them to hide their authentic quirks and preferences.

Through CBT, individuals can identify and challenge these distortions. Techniques such as cognitive restructuring help people reframe their thoughts more balanced and realistic. One can learn to accept that making mistakes is part of being human rather than believing they must always be perfect. This acceptance reduces the pressure to conform to unrealistic standards and encourages a more authentic presentation of oneself. Being neurodiverse and embracing your quirkiness means celebrating the unique perspectives and behaviors that make you who you are. It involves recognizing that what society may label as "quirky" or "different" are valuable aspects of your identity. Embracing your quirkiness allows you to live authentically, appreciating your special interests, deep passions, and unique ways of thinking. This self-acceptance empowers you to navigate the world on your terms, fostering resilience and confidence. By embracing these traits, you contribute to the richness of human diversity, challenging conventional norms and inspiring others to appreciate the beauty in neurodiversity. It's about finding strength in your individuality and creating a life that reflects your true self without conforming to neurotypical standards. I have learned that the parts of my personality I have been hiding for decades are the aspects the ones closest to me love most. You may be surprised by the beautiful discoveries unmasking may bring.

Here's a practice for fostering a more compassionate and accepting view of oneself, essential for those seeking to unmask and live authentically.

Cognitive Restructuring Practice

This practice aims to help you recognize and transform negative self-talk into more compassionate and accepting thoughts.

Steps:

1. **Identify Negative Thoughts** :

    ◦ Throughout your day, take note of any negative thoughts you have about yourself. Write them down in a journal. These might be thoughts like, "I'm not good enough," "I always mess things up," or "People don't like me."

3. **Examine the Evidence** :

    ◦ For each negative thought, ask yourself:

        ▪ What evidence supports this thought?

        ▪ What evidence contradicts this thought?

    ◦ Write down both the supporting and contradicting evidence.

5. **Challenge the Negative Thought** :

    ◦ Consider the contradicting evidence and ask yourself:

        ▪ Is this thought formed from facts or feelings?

        ▪ Am I overgeneralizing or catastrophizing?

        ▪ What would I say to a friend who had this thought about themselves?

7. **Reframe the Thought** :

   ◦ Develop a more balanced and compassionate thought to replace the negative one. For example:

      ▪ Negative thought: "I'm not good enough."

      ▪ Reframed Thought: "I'm doing my best, and that is enough. Everyone has strengths and weaknesses."

9. **Practice Self-Compassion** :

   ◦ Incorporate self-compassionate statements into your daily routine. When you notice a negative thought, consciously replace it with compassion. Examples include:

      ▪ "It's okay to make mistakes; they are part of learning."

      ▪ "I am worthy of love and acceptance just as I am."

      ▪ "I have distinctive strengths and qualities that make me unique."

11. **Visualize Success** :

   ◦ Spend a few minutes each day visualizing yourself handling situations where you typically experience negative self-talk. Imagine yourself responding with self-compassion and confidence.

13. **Reflect and Reinforce** :

   ◦ At the end of each week, reflect on your progress. Write down instances where you successfully reframed negative thoughts and responded with self-compassion.

   ◦ Reinforce your efforts by acknowledging your progress and setting small, achievable goals for continued practice.

Example in Practice

1. **Identify Negative Thought** : "I always mess things up in social situations."

2. **Examine the Evidence** :
   - Supporting evidence: "I felt awkward at the party last week."
   - Contradicting evidence: "I had a great conversation with my colleagues yesterday, and they seemed to enjoy it."

4. **Challenge the Negative Thought** :
   - "I may have felt awkward at the party, but that docsn't mean I always mess things up. I positively interacted with my colleague, which shows I can have successful social interactions."

6. **Reframe the Thought** :
   - "I might feel awkward sometimes, but I can have meaningful and enjoyable conversations."

8. **Practice Self-Compassion** :
   - "It's normal to feel awkward sometimes. Everyone does. What matters is that I keep trying and learning."

10. **Visualize Success** :
    - Visualize yourself at the next social event, feeling confident and engaging in pleasant conversations.

12. **Reflect and Reinforce** :
    - "This week, I felt more confident when I reminded myself of my successful conversations. I will remain

dedicated to focusing on my strengths and practicing self-compassion."

Benefits:

- **Reduces Negative Self-Talk** : Helps diminish harmful and unproductive thought patterns.

- **Builds Self-Acceptance** : Encourages a more compassionate and realistic view of oneself.

- **Promotes Authenticity** : Supports unmasking and living more authentically by fostering self-acceptance and confidence.

- **Enhances Emotional Well-Being** : Contributes to overall mental health by reducing anxiety and depression associated with negative self-perceptions.

By regularly practicing cognitive restructuring, you can develop a more compassionate and accepting view of yourself, enabling you to live more authentically and confidently.

As individuals restructure their cognitive distortions, they often find it easier to embrace their true selves. Authenticity becomes more attainable when one no longer feels compelled to meet impossible standards or suppress natural inclinations. This process of cognitive restructuring fosters a more compassionate and accepting view of oneself, which is essential for those seeking to unmask and live authentically. The shift from self-criticism to self-compassion allows for greater freedom in expressing one's true identity.

Mindfulness activities also significantly influence the journey towards emotional regulation and self-acceptance. Cultivating present-moment awareness through mindfulness helps individuals stay grounded in the here and now. This practice is especially beneficial for those prone to anxiety about future social interactions or regret over past ones. Focusing on the present moment can reduce the mental noise that often fuels masking behaviors.

Mindfulness enhances emotional regulation by helping individuals observe their thoughts and feelings without immediate reaction. This non-judgmental observation creates a space between the stimulus and the response, allowing for more thoughtful and authentic reactions. For instance, rather than immediately masking a feeling of sadness to appear composed, a person practicing mindfulness might acknowledge the sadness and allow themselves to express it appropriately. This approach leads to more genuine interactions and reduces the strain of constant masking.

Moreover, mindfulness practices encourage self-acceptance. Regularly engaging in mindfulness allows individuals to observe their thoughts and emotions without judgment. This practice fosters a kinder and more accepting attitude towards oneself. Instead of striving to meet external expectations, individuals accept their inherent worth and uniqueness. This self-acceptance is crucial for unmasking, as it allows people to feel secure in showing their true selves, imperfections, and all.

Connecting with one's inner child is another profound benefit of mindfulness. Masking behaviors often develop to protect oneself from past hurts and vulnerabilities experienced during childhood. Mindfulness techniques, including guided imagery or meditation, can help individuals reconnect with their inner child and address these old wounds. Individuals can build a stronger, more integrated sense of identity by acknowledging and healing these parts of themselves.

Revisiting the inner child allows for greater compassion and understanding of oneself. When individuals connect with their past's innocent, playful aspects, they can release the need to constantly present a guarded or altered version of themselves. This connection promotes healing and authenticity, as it resolves some of the deep-seated reasons for masking. As individuals nurture their inner child, they become more open to expressing their true selves in the present.

Finally, incorporating CBT techniques alongside mindfulness offers a comprehensive approach to authentically navigating social situations. Practical tools from CBT, such as thought records and behavioral experiments, provide structured ways to challenge unhelpful beliefs and test new, authentic behaviors. For example, individuals can use thought records to track instances where they need to mask and analyze the underlying thoughts and outcomes. This analysis can reveal patterns and areas for change.

Another CBT tool is behavioral experiments, which encourage individuals to try new ways of interacting without masking and observing the results. These experiments can be enlightening, often demonstrating that the feared adverse outcomes of being authentic are less likely than anticipated. By combining mindfulness's introspective work with CBT's actionable strategies, individuals can make meaningful progress in their unmasking journey. This dual approach equips them with the self-awareness and practical skills to navigate life authentically.

Balancing Self-Help Techniques with Professional Guidance

Balancing self-help techniques with professional guidance is crucial on the journey of unmasking for those with autism and ADHD. An essential aspect of this balance involves complementing therapy with self-reflection. Self-reflection enables individuals to enhance their self-awareness, a key element in the unmasking process. When paired with professional treatment, self-reflection helps one better understand personal behaviors and emotions, fostering a deeper connection to one's true self.

Journaling is a powerful tool for looking inward and tracking progress during unmasking. By writing down thoughts and experiences, individuals can gain valuable awareness of their emotional responses and behavioral patterns. This practice not only aids in self-discovery but also provides a tangible record of growth over time. Therapists can use journal entries to identify recurring themes and tailor their guidance accordingly, making each therapy session more effective.

Moreover, journaling allows for a safe space to explore feelings without judgment. For late-diagnosed autistic adults and those with ADHD, this reflective practice encourages authenticity and reduces the pressure to mask their true selves. By revisiting journal entries, individuals can celebrate milestones and recognize areas needing further work, thus enhancing their therapeutic experience.

Seeking support from like-minded individuals can significantly complement professional therapy. Joining groups or communities where members share similar experiences can produce a sense of belonging and validation. These peer interactions create an environment where individuals feel understood and less isolated in their journey. Sharing stories and challenges with peers can offer new perspectives and coping strategies that reinforce the lessons learned in therapy.

Engaging with a support network helps bridge the gap between professional advice and real-life application. Like-minded peers can provide practical suggestions on navigating daily challenges, thus enriching the individual's ability to unmask authentically. Moreover, the encouragement received from such communities often serves as motivation to continue the hard work initiated in therapy.

Building a support network is essential for reinforcing therapeutic progress and encouraging continued growth. Whether through formal support groups or informal connections, these networks provide a foundation of trust and understanding. In such settings, individuals are more likely to express themselves freely and seek advice without fear of judgment.

A strong support network offers a consistent source of encouragement and accountability. When therapy sessions end, these connections help maintain momentum by reminding individuals of their goals and progress. Coaches, mentors, or friends within the network can provide ongoing feedback and assist in implementing therapeutic strategies in everyday life.

Real-Life Examples of Therapy Successes

Imagine myself, a woman diagnosed with autism in my forties. Feeling lost and overwhelmed by my newly discovered identity, I sought professional support. Through regular therapy sessions, I learned to recognize and understand the behaviors I had masked for years. My therapist guided me through exercises that helped me realize my triggers and develop strategies for coping. Over time, I began to feel more comfortable embracing my genuine self, acknowledging that my differences were strengths rather than flaws.

Similarly, consider Alex, an individual with ADHD who struggled with chronic disorganization and impulsivity. By engaging in therapy, he started to unravel the patterns that led to his challenges. His therapist used practical tools and cognitive-behavioral techniques to help him create structure in his daily life. Slowly, Alex noticed significant improvements in his ability to focus and manage tasks. These personal accounts highlight how therapy can empower individuals to transform their lives by providing tailored support.

Moreover, John's experience showcases the depths of breakthroughs possible within therapy. Diagnosed late with autism, he initially felt isolated and misunderstood. Working closely with a therapist specializing in neurodiversity, he reached a pivotal moment where he finally connected with his inner child. This breakthrough allowed John to embrace his past experiences and understand how they shaped his present. Witnessing such profound progress inspires others to seek therapy and reinforces the belief that meaningful change is achievable.

Another vivid example comes from Maria, who had long masked her ADHD symptoms at work by adopting exhausting coping mechanisms. Therapy sessions offered her a safe space to unpack these behaviors and explore healthier alternatives. With professional guidance, Maria implemented new strategies to manage her workload without compromising her well-being. Over time, she experienced less burnout and greater satisfaction in her career. These stories offer concrete evidence of the positive shifts therapy can instigate, motivating individuals to pursue their own unmasking journeys.

Incorporating feedback from those who've benefitted from therapy underscores its positive impact. For instance, Jane shared how therapy helped her navigate the complexities of living with both autism and ADHD. Her therapist's empathetic approach made her feel seen and heard, providing her with tools to better understand herself. Jane's testimony reflects therapists' critical role in validating and supporting their clients' experiences, enhancing readers' trust in seeking professional help.

Paul's reflections provide additional insights into therapy's benefits. Initially skeptical, he found that discussing his ADHD-related challenges with his therapist yielded practical solutions that improved his daily functioning. Positive feedback like Paul's is an encouraging reminder of therapy's tangible benefits, reinforcing the value of investing in one's mental health. Such authentic accounts strengthen the narrative that professional support is worthwhile and transformative.

Hearing from peers about their therapy experiences further normalizes seeking help and builds community. Emily, for example, shared her journey in group therapy sessions designed for adults with late-diagnosed autism. Listening to similar struggles and triumphs among her peers made her feel less alone. The collective experience fostered a supportive environment where members could exchange advice and encouragement, emphasizing the communal aspect of therapeutic progress.

Additionally, Sam's story highlights the importance of shared experiences. Attending ADHD support groups, he found solace in connecting with others who understood his struggles. The camaraderie in these settings often mirrored the supportive dynamic seen in individual therapy, underscoring the normalization of seeking help. Stories like Sam's demonstrate the power of peer support in complementing professional treatment, creating a holistic approach to unmasking and self-acceptance.

Furthermore, Melissa's journey emphasizes the benefits of open dialogue within a therapeutic setting. She recounted how sharing her experiences with fellow therapy attendees created a sense of solidarity and mutual understanding. This peer interaction affirmed that seeking help was a step towards healing rather than a sign of weakness. Hearing varied therapy success stories can reduce stigma and encourage more individuals to pursue the support they need.

Lessons Learned and Next Steps in Unmasking

Therapy serves as a powerful instrument in the journey toward unmasking and healing for late-diagnosed autistic adults and individuals with ADHD. This chapter has explored how finding the right therapist specializing in autism and ADHD can significantly enhance this process. We've discussed the importance of therapists who understand the specific challenges faced by late-diagnosed individuals, the benefits of tailored therapeutic approaches, and the necessity of establishing trust within the therapeutic relationship.

When we began, we talked about the unique hurdles that late-diagnosed individuals face, such as years of masking behaviors and internalized stigma. With professional guidance, these patterns can be effectively dismantled, allowing for a more authentic expression of self. Such personalized care validates the client's experiences and fosters a supportive environment where growth and healing are possible.

However, readers should remember that finding the right therapist involves carefully considering the therapist's expertise, credentials, and experience with neurodiverse clients. This ensures that the support received is relevant, informed, and effective. Individuals need to assess these factors before committing to a therapist, as the foundation of empathy and understanding is crucial to the success of therapy.

The broader implications of this approach are significant. When late-diagnosed individuals receive appropriate and compassionate care, they experience greater self-acceptance, reduced mental strain from constant masking, and improved quality of life. This shift benefits individuals and their interactions with the world, fostering a more inclusive society that values neurodiversity.

As we conclude this discussion, reflecting on how therapy's role extends beyond symptom management is essential. It offers a pathway to deeper self-understanding and acceptance, empowering individuals to live more authentically. Counseling provides a safe space for exploring one's true identity, free from societal pressures and expectations.

Looking forward, consider the ongoing nature of this journey. Unmasking and healing are continuous processes that require patience, dedication, and the proper support. Future chapters will explore more tools and strategies to help you embrace your true self. Remember that this path is uniquely yours, and while challenging, it is also rewarding.

In essence, therapy is a cornerstone in the unmasking journey, providing the necessary support to navigate this transformative process. As you move ahead, hold onto the belief that authenticity and self-acceptance are within reach with the proper guidance. The following steps in this journey will build upon this foundation, helping you connect more deeply with your inner child and embrace the fullness of your unique identity.

Building a Supportive Environment: Family and Friends

C reating a supportive environment for unmasking and authenticity is vital for late-diagnosed autistic adults and individuals with ADHD. Family and friends need to understand the concept of masking, which involves hiding actual behaviors and emotions to fit societal norms. This chapter investigates how educating loved ones about masking can foster empathy and support. It offers insights into recognizing and understanding the profound impact that masking has on individuals.

The chapter explores strategies for developing an accepting environment where individuals feel secure to convey their true selves. It emphasizes the importance of patience, active listening, and emotional encouragement from family and friends. Discussions will include practical steps for promoting acceptance and empathy, managing difficult conversations, setting boundaries, and providing ongoing reassurance. By the end, readers will understand how to nurture a supportive environment that encourages self-acceptance and authenticity.

Educating Family and Friends about Masking

Understanding the concept of masking is crucial for family and friends who aim to effectively support their loved ones with autism or ADHD. Masking involves camouflaging one's true self to fit social norms, often leading to physical and emotional exhaustion. This behavior, which may be misunderstood as shyness or introversion, is a coping mechanism that helps avoid negative social experiences. By recognizing these subtle behaviors, family and friends can better empathize and offer the proper support.

Awareness of masking goes beyond recognizing these behaviors; it requires understanding their profound impact. Individuals who mask often do so to avoid social exclusion or judgment, but this constant facade can cause significant mental strain. Understanding this, family members and friends can appreciate the effort involved in masking and the courage it takes to unmask. Supportive environments are characterized by patience, empathy, and a willingness to learn about the challenges presented by those who mask.

Creating an open and accepting environment is vital. Encouraging an atmosphere where individuals feel safe to convey their true selves without fear of criticism fosters trust and mutual respect. Family and friends should practice active listening, showing genuine interest in their loved one's experiences. This approach validates their feelings and promotes stronger relationships built on acceptance and understanding.

Empathy plays a critical role in supporting unmasking. It involves seeing the world from another person's perspective and understanding their emotional journey. Encouraging empathy within the family can help create a nurturing surrounding where individuals feel understood and accepted. Sharing educational resources about masking can also help family members better understand what their loved ones are experiencing.

Acceptance is equally essential. Family and friends must show unconditional love and support, regardless of whether their loved one is masking or unmasking. Acceptance helps reduce the pressure to conform to societal expectations and encourages authenticity. When individuals feel accepted as they are, they are more likely to embark on the journey of unmasking, knowing they have a reliable support system.

Honest conversations about the challenges and benefits of unmasking are necessary. These dialogues help clarify any misconceptions and why unmasking is a significant step towards self-acceptance. Holding these discussions in a safe, non-judgmental space allows individuals to openly voice their concerns and fears. It also allows family and friends to express their support and commitment to being allies in the unmasking process.

Promoting active listening and validation during these conversations is essential. Active listening involves paying full attention, reflecting on what is said, and responding thoughtfully. Validation confirms that the individual's feelings and thoughts are influential and respected. This practice can significantly increase confidence and willingness to unmask, knowing their emotions are acknowledged and supported.

Supporting individuals in their unmasking journey requires practical guidance and emotional encouragement. Families can join support groups to learn strategies and share stories that resonate with others in similar situations. Providing consistent reassurance and positive reinforcement can help individuals feel less vulnerable as they gradually reveal their authentic selves. This ongoing support can make the transition smoother and less daunting.

Offering encouragement and reassurance throughout the unmasking process is crucial. It involves celebrating small victories and acknowledging the bravery required to be genuine. Consistent encouragement reinforces the idea that being authentic is okay and reduces the anxiety associated with unmasking. Reassurance can come in the form of verbal affirmations, acts of kindness, and being present when needed.

Collaborating with individuals to establish boundaries and preferences during unmasking is also essential. Respecting personal boundaries ensures that the unmasking process is done at a comfortable pace. Preferences regarding social interactions, communication styles, and expressions of authenticity should be discussed and honored. This collaboration fosters a sense of agency and control over the unmasking journey, making it a more empowering experience.

Establishing guidelines for communication and interaction can further enhance support. Guidelines might include:

- Setting aside regular times for check-ins.
- Creating signals for when someone feels overwhelmed.
- Agreeing on how to handle difficult social situations.

Clear and respectful communication helps prevent misunderstandings and ensures everyone affected is on the same page.

Navigating Difficult Conversations

Navigating difficult conversations around unmasking can be a delicate and complex process. It involves expressing deeply personal experiences and encouraging understanding among family and friends who might not fully grasp the nuances of masking behaviors. Creating a space where open dialogue is welcomed and misunderstandings are gently addressed is essential.

Encouraging open communication is the cornerstone of navigating these challenging discussions. When discussing unmasking, it's vital to approach conversations with empathy and patience. Begin by explaining the concept of masking in simple terms, emphasizing how it impacts daily life. Sharing personal anecdotes can help illustrate how masking has affected your sense of self and interactions with others. For instance, you might describe a situation where you felt compelled to hide your true feelings or behaviors due to societal expectations or peer pressure.

Allowing family and friends to ask questions and share their perspectives is crucial. This two-way communication fosters a deeper understanding and allows for the exchange of honest ideas and emotions. Encouraging them to express their initial reactions or concerns without judgment helps build a foundation of trust. Remember, this is a learning journey for everyone involved; giving them the space to process new information at their own pace is vital.

Establishing safe spaces for discussing sensitive topics related to unmasking is another significant aspect of effective conversation. Select a comfortable setting free from distractions, where all parties feel secure to speak openly. Setting ground rules for these discussions can help maintain a respectful and supportive atmosphere. For example, agreeing that everyone will listen actively without interrupting can significantly enhance the quality of the conversation.

When approaching sensitive topics, using "I" rather than "you" statements can prevent defensiveness and promote understanding. For example, saying, "I feel overwhelmed when I have to mask my behaviors," is more effective than "You don't understand what it's like for me." This subtle shift can substantially affect how your message is received. Additionally, validating each other's feelings, even when there is disagreement, reinforces the importance of mutual respect and empathy.

Promoting effective communication strategies to express needs and concerns involves honing specific skills to benefit both parties. Active listening, which includes making eye contact, nodding, and summarizing the other person's words, shows that you value their input. This practice can reduce miscommunications and promote a more meaningful dialogue.

Incorporating mindfulness into your communication can also be highly beneficial. Mindfulness encourages staying present and fully engaged during conversations. Methods such as taking deep breaths before responding, noticing emotional triggers, and pausing to reflect on your words can help keep discussions calm and constructive (Gillis Chapman, S., 2019). Practicing these strategies can lead to a more empathetic and understanding communication style.

Managing varying reactions from family and friends is an inevitable part of discussing unmasking. Reactions can range from supportive and curious to confused or resistant. Preparing for these different responses and approaching them with compassion is vital. Understanding that resistance often stems from unfamiliarity or fear of change can help you respond with patience.

Coping mechanisms for dealing with negative responses or resistance are essential for maintaining emotional well-being. One effective strategy is boundary-setting. Clearly defining acceptable behavior in these conversations helps protect your mental health. For instance, if a family member frequently interrupts or dismisses your experiences, calmly stating that such interruptions make it hard for you to share can be a way to assert your boundaries without escalating tension.

Another coping mechanism is seeking support from trusted individuals outside the immediate circle involved in the conversation. Friends, support groups, or therapists can provide a safe space to vent and receive validation and advice. This external support can bolster your resilience and offer different perspectives on handling challenging interactions.

Strategies for setting boundaries and maintaining self-care during difficult conversations cannot be overstated. Establishing clear limits on the duration and frequency of these conversations can prevent burnout. For example, limiting intense discussions to one hour or determining specific times to revisit the topic can be helpful.

Communicating these boundaries clearly to family and friends ensures everyone respects your need for space and recovery.

Engaging in relaxing activities before and after the conversation is a self-care practice that can help manage stress. Whether practicing yoga, journaling, or spending time in nature, these activities remind you to prioritize your well-being amidst challenging discussions. Balancing these strategies with openness to dialogue creates a healthier and more sustainable way to navigate these crucial conversations.

Building trust through honest and vulnerable communication is fundamental to fostering supportive relationships. Trust grows when both parties are willing to share their thoughts and feelings openly. This honesty should extend to acknowledging when specific topics or comments cause discomfort and recognizing moments of shared empathy and understanding.

Establishing mutual respect and understanding in relationships involves recognizing and appreciating each other's communication efforts. Acknowledging the challenges of changing long-held perceptions about masking can foster a collaborative spirit. Expressing gratitude for family and friends' willingness to learn and adapt demonstrates your appreciation for their support.

Strengthening emotional connections by sharing personal experiences can deepen understanding and empathy. Sharing stories about how masking has impacted your life helps paint a vivid picture of your experiences. It also allows your loved ones to see the world from your perspective, promoting a deeper emotional connection rooted in authenticity.

Creating Inclusive and Understanding Home Environments

Creating an inclusive and understanding home environment is essential for promoting authenticity and self-expression, particularly for late-diagnosed autistic adults and individuals with ADHD. Establishing a safe and welcoming space within the home encourages members to be their genuine selves without fear of judgment or criticism. This process begins with open communication and active listening. Families should create opportunities for honest discussions where each member feels heard and valued. Recognizing and validating each individual's unique experiences and perspectives is vital.

Designing physical environments that reflect and honor personal identities can further enhance a sense of belonging. Personal spaces should be tailored to meet sensory needs and preferences. For instance, some individuals may prefer quiet, dimly lit areas, while others might thrive in brighter, more stimulating surroundings. Encouraging family members to personalize their living spaces with items that hold personal significance can significantly boost their comfort and confidence to express their true selves.

Routine implementation that prioritizes mental and emotional well-being is another cornerstone of supportive home environments. Predictable routines provide stability, reduce anxiety, and create a sense of security. Incorporating activities that promote relaxation, such as mindfulness exercises or creative hobbies, supports emotional balance. Also, setting aside time for regular family check-ins ensures that everyone remains connected and attuned to each other's evolving needs and emotions.

Cultural sensitivity is crucial in fostering a supportive and inclusive atmosphere. Respecting individual differences and cultural backgrounds within the home helps create an environment where diversity is celebrated rather than merely tolerated. Being mindful of cultural norms that impact expressions of authenticity allows family members to navigate their identities while staying true to their cultural heritage. It is essential to offer support when these norms pose challenges to self-expression, ensuring every member feels understood and accepted.

Celebrating diversity and promoting inclusivity within family dynamics goes hand-in-hand with cultural sensitivity. Activities like cultural celebrations, shared storytelling, and exploring diverse traditions together can reinforce the value of each person's background. Embracing various perspectives enriches the family unit, creating a vibrant mosaic of experiences and viewpoints. This approach nurtures mutual respect and admiration among family members, encouraging authentic self-expression.

Emotional support is crucial in aiding individuals to unmask and embrace their true selves. Providing consistent emotional encouragement during moments of self-discovery fosters resilience and confidence. Family members should strive to offer practical assistance and understanding, especially during times of vulnerability. Small gestures of support, whether through kind words, active listening, or simply being present, can significantly impact someone's journey toward authenticity.

Encouraging self-expression through creative outlets and activities is equally important. Creativity offers a non-verbal avenue for expressing feelings and thoughts that might be problematic. Whether drawing, writing, music, or any other art form, these creative pursuits can be powerful tools for personal reflection and expression. Sharing these creative endeavors within the family can strengthen bonds and deepen mutual understanding.

Community and Peer Support Groups

Encouraging participation in supportive communities and peer groups is a critical first step toward creating a supportive environment for unmasking. Community and peer support groups provide a unique space where individuals can join, share their experiences, and feel understood, reducing feelings of isolation. These groups offer validation and acceptance, crucial elements that help individuals gain confidence to unmask and embrace their genuine selves without fear of judgment.

Finding like-minded individuals with similar experiences and challenges is essential in fostering a sense of belonging. When people connect within these support groups, they often find solace in knowing they are not alone in their struggles. This connection can be comforting and empowering, allowing them to open up about their experiences more freely. Bonding with people who understand what it means to mask and the challenges of unmasking creates a network of trust and mutual respect.

Building a network of support that offers guidance and solidarity in the unmasking journey is vital for sustained emotional health. A solid support network acts as a safety net during doubt or difficulty. Through regular interactions and shared activities, these groups develop deep bonds that provide strength and encouragement. This collective strength can be instrumental when facing societal pressures or personal insecurities, helping individuals stay committed to authenticity.

Utilizing community connections to exchange stories and insights on unmasking is another crucial aspect of fostering a supportive environment. Personal stories serve as powerful tools for learning and growth. By hearing others' journeys, individuals can gain new perspectives on their own experiences, which can be incredibly enlightening and motivating. Sharing stories helps normalize unmasked behaviors and reduces the stigma of being different.

Learning from others' experiences and gaining perspectives on authenticity contributes to personal development. Being part of a peer group allows individuals to tap into a wealth of shared wisdom. Members can provide practical advice and emotional support based on their personal journeys. This shared knowledge helps individuals navigate their paths more effectively, potentially avoiding pitfalls others have faced and finding new strategies for staying true to themselves.

One of the most profound benefits of peer groups is providing mutual encouragement and empowerment within a supportive social circle. Positive reinforcement from peers reinforces self-worth and promotes resilience. Knowing that others believe in their ability to live authentically can motivate individuals to continue unmasking despite external challenges. In this way, peer support groups nurture a culture of empowerment, enabling members to lift each other up consistently.

Establishing secure and nurturing environments within community settings is paramount for effective unmasking. Safety and security are foundational to fostering an atmosphere where individuals feel comfortable being vulnerable. Support groups must prioritize creating spaces where members can show their true selves without fear of retribution or exclusion. Such environments act as sanctuaries where authenticity is not only accepted but celebrated.

Promoting confidentiality and trust within peer support groups is essential to maintaining these safe spaces. Confidentiality ensures that what is shared within the group stays within the group, fostering an atmosphere of trust. Trust is the bedrock of any support system, enabling individuals to open up about deeply personal experiences. Facilitators and group members alike have a role in nurturing this trust by respecting boundaries and upholding the group's guidelines on privacy and respect.

Offering a forum for individuals to reveal themselves without fear of judgment or discrimination is instrumental in encouraging genuine self-expression. When people know they will be met with empathy and understanding, they are increasingly likely to share openly. This openness leads to a richer sharing of ideas and experiences, adding to the overall growth and supportiveness of the group. Support groups can become inclusive spaces where every member feels valued by ensuring no one feels marginalized or judged.

The role of community and peer support groups extends beyond simply providing a venue for interaction; they serve as catalysts for more profound personal transformation. These groups foster a culture of acceptance and understanding, helping individuals navigate the complex unmasking process. By participating in such groups, individuals are supported and empowered to support others, creating a cycle of mutual growth and understanding.

Involvement in peer support groups encourages a shift from isolation to community, transforming lived experiences into collective resilience. The narratives shared within these groups highlight individual struggles and triumphs, showcasing the strength found in vulnerability. As members learn from each other, they build a collective knowledge base that supports continuous learning and personal development.

Summary of Building a Supportive Environment

Throughout this chapter, we have explored the significance of creating a supportive environment for unmasking and fostering authenticity. We have delved into the concept of masking, its profound impact on individuals, and the vital role that family and friends play in this journey. Understanding, empathy, and acceptance are the cornerstones of such an environment, and these traits help build stronger, more meaningful relationships.

Returning to our initial discussion, we emphasized educating family and friends about masking behaviors. Recognizing these behaviors is only the first step; understanding the emotional strain behind them is equally important. As we reflect on what has been discussed, it becomes clear that developing patience and empathy towards loved ones who mask is crucial. These qualities facilitate unmasking and reinforce the courage it takes to reveal one's true self.

Our current position underscores the importance of fostering open communication and mutual respect. Active listening, validation, and setting safe dialogue spaces are essential practices. These strategies enable individuals to voice their thoughts and concerns without judgment or criticism. Through such honest conversations, more profound understanding and trust are nurtured.

However, some readers might be concerned about navigating these interactions effectively. Misunderstandings may arise, and reactions can vary widely among family members and friends. Preparing for diverse responses and practicing compassion can help manage potential challenges. It's crucial to remember that resistance often stems from unfamiliarity or fear of change. Patience and persistence in educating and supporting loved ones go a long way in overcoming these hurdles.

Fostering a supportive environment has far-reaching consequences. When individuals feel understood and accepted, they are more likely to embrace their authentic selves and contribute positively to their communities. This ripple effect can gradually lead to more inclusive societies where diversity is celebrated and differences are respected.

As we conclude, consider the transformative power of empathy and acceptance in your own life. Reflect on your relationships and how you can further support those around you in their journey towards unmasking. By cultivating these qualities, we can help create environments where everyone feels free to be their true selves.

The journey of unmasking and embracing authenticity is ongoing and begins with small, empathetic steps. Let this chapter inspire you to foster such an environment within your circles, paving the way for deeper connections and genuine self-expression. In doing so, we move towards a world where authenticity is appreciated and encouraged.

Workplace Realities: Navigating Professional Life

N avigating professional life can be a complex journey, especially for late-diagnosed autistic adults and individuals with ADHD who are learning to unmask and embrace their true selves. Balancing the demands of work while staying authentic involves understanding legal protections, advocating for necessary accommodations, and fostering inclusive environments. This chapter explores these intricacies with empathy and clarity, offering practical strategies for thriving in the workplace without compromising one's identity.

This chapter will explore essential topics, such as understanding your legal rights under the Americans with Disabilities Act (ADA) and how it safeguards against discrimination. We'll discuss the importance of requesting reasonable accommodations tailored to individual needs and how clear, concise communication can facilitate these requests. Additionally, we will explore recognizing and addressing workplace discrimination, emphasizing the importance of familiarizing oneself with company policies and utilizing available resources for support. Finally, we'll highlight ways to enhance workplace inclusivity through better communication, regular feedback, and building a supportive culture that values neurodiversity. By the end of this chapter, readers will have actionable insights to navigate their professional lives more confidently and authentically.

Understanding Legal Rights and Workplace Accommodations

Understanding legal rights and workplace accommodations is essential for neurodiverse individuals seeking to unmask and embrace their authentic selves professionally. One critical protection for these individuals is the Americans with Disabilities Act (ADA). The ADA prevents prejudice against persons with disabilities in various areas, including employment. It ensures that employers cannot discriminate based on a person's disability and must provide reasonable accommodations to allow employees to accomplish their jobs effectively.

It's essential to know that the ADA covers any workplace with 15 or more employees. Under the ADA, a person with a disability is a physical or mental impairment substantially restricting one or more vital life activities. This broad definition includes neurodiverse conditions such as autism and ADHD. Employers must make equitable accommodations unless doing so would cause undue hardship to the business, ensuring that neurodiverse employees can work in an environment tailored to their needs.

Knowing how to request reasonable accommodations is crucial in supporting unmasking efforts in the workplace. Employees should first identify the specific needs related to their condition. For example, those with sensory sensitivities might benefit from noise-canceling headphones or a quieter workspace. Flexible schedules can also be highly advantageous for individuals with ADHD who may experience fluctuations in focus and productivity throughout the day.

Clear and concise communication is vital when making a request. It's essential to explain the nature of the disability and how it affects job performance, then suggest specific accommodations that would help. Providing documentation from a healthcare provider can also support the request. Employers are generally receptive to such requests when they understand how these adjustments can enhance employee performance and well-being.

Recognizing discrimination and advocating for one's rights requires a thorough understanding of workplace policies and procedures. Discrimination can manifest in various forms, from outright refusal to provide accommodations to subtle biases that create a hostile work environment. Knowing the symptoms of discrimination and having a zero-tolerance approach toward it is vital for neurodiverse individuals and their allies.

Employees should familiarize themselves with their company's anti-discrimination policies and reporting procedures. Many organizations have designated staff or departments responsible for handling discrimination complaints, such as HR. Documenting instances of discrimination meticulously and presenting them as evidence when filing a complaint can strengthen the case. Utilizing resources such as the Equal Employment Opportunity Commission (EEOC) can also be beneficial, as they provide guidance and a formal process for addressing workplace discrimination.

Implementing communication support in the workplace promotes inclusivity and understanding. Clear instructions and feedback are invaluable tools for neurodivergent employees, helping them navigate tasks and expectations more effectively. Employers can adopt strategies like providing written instructions, using visual aids, or breaking down tasks into smaller, manageable steps.

Regular feedback sessions can also foster a supportive environment. Constructive feedback helps employees understand their performance and areas for improvement without feeling overwhelmed. Additionally, open lines of communication between supervisors and neurodiverse employees encourage ongoing dialogue about needs and accommodations, making it easier to address issues promptly and adapt strategies as necessary.

Workplace accommodations extend beyond modifying physical environments; they encompass creating a culture of acceptance and inclusivity. Providing sensory-friendly workplaces involves practical changes, like adjusting lighting or minimizing background noise. Flexible schedules grants employees to work during their most productive hours, thus enhancing both performance and job satisfaction. These accommodations show that the employer values diversity and is committed to supporting all employees.

It is equally important to promote understanding and acceptance of neurodiversity among colleagues. Peer education and awareness programs can demystify neurodiverse conditions, reducing stigma and fostering empathy. Encouraging team-building activities and inclusive practices ensures that neurodiverse employees feel understood and supported by their peers.

Navigating the decision to disclose neurodivergence at work can be challenging. Disclosure is a personal choice, and weighing the benefits and risks is essential. On one hand, revealing a diagnosis can lead to better support and accommodations, creating a more comfortable work environment. It can also foster openness and understanding, encouraging others to share their challenges and creating a more inclusive workplace culture.

However, disclosure has potential downsides. Fear of judgment or bias may deter some individuals from revealing their condition. Concerns about privacy and the impact on professional relationships are valid and must be considered carefully. Each individual's circumstances are unique, and weighing these components will aid in making an educated decision.

Enhancing Communication Skills for Expressing Needs and Fostering Workplace Inclusion

Enhancing communication skills is pivotal for expressing needs and fostering workplace inclusion, especially for late-diagnosed autistic adults and individuals with ADHD. Practicing assertive communication is a good starting point. Assertive communication involves expressing your needs, wants, and boundaries clearly and respectfully. This means speaking up about what you need to thrive at work—whether it's a quieter workspace, flexible deadlines, or specific instructions. Being assertive means advocating for yourself without feeling guilty or afraid of judgment.

One technique for practicing assertive communication is using "I" statements. For example, saying, "I need a quiet space to focus better," instead of "You are too loud." This way, the focus remains on your needs rather than blaming others. Another method is preparing for conversations by writing down key points beforehand. This can help ensure you cover all essential topics and maintain focus during discussions. Role-playing scenarios with a friend or therapist can also provide practice in a safe environment before applying these skills at work (Hopler, W., 2022).

Assertive communication not only helps articulate needs but also establishes boundaries. Clear boundaries prevent misunderstandings and reduce stress. It's important to communicate these boundaries early and reinforce them as needed. For instance, let your team know if you prefer not to answer emails after working hours. Setting these boundaries enables you to protect your personal time and mental health, making it easier to manage sensory overload and other challenges common among neurodiverse individuals.

Establishing relationships with colleagues and mentors is another crucial step in building a supportive network. Positive relationships encourage a sense of belonging and foster an inclusive work culture. Start by seeking out like-minded colleagues who may share similar experiences. Joining employee resource groups focused on neurodiversity can be an excellent way to meet people who understand your challenges and can offer support.

Mentorship is particularly beneficial. A mentor can supply guidance, share their experiences, and help navigate workplace dynamics. Look for mentors who appreciate diversity and are willing to invest in your growth. Mentors can often bridge gaps, advocating on your behalf when necessary and offering strategies to handle difficult situations. This kind of support network empowers you, providing insights and encouragement needed to succeed professionally.

Building relationships doesn't stop at finding a mentor. It's equally important to cultivate strong connections with peers. Informal gatherings, such as coffee breaks or lunch outings, can help strengthen bonds outside of formal work settings. These interactions build trust and camaraderie, making it easier to collaborate and seek support when required. Being open about your experiences can encourage others to share theirs, creating an environment of mutual understanding and respect.

Setting boundaries and prioritizing self-care are vital for managing stress and sensory overload. Self-care practices include regular breaks, mindfulness exercises, or ensuring a suitable work environment. Communicating these needs with your team can help everyone understand why certain adjustments are necessary. Explain how small changes can significantly impact your productivity and well-being.

Developing coping mechanisms for stress is another part of self-care. Techniques such as deep breathing, meditation, or playing soothing music can help manage anxiety. Additionally, having a designated quiet workplace space to retreat during overwhelming moments can make a big difference. It's essential to experiment with various strategies to find what works best for you and to communicate these preferences to your supervisor.

Prioritizing self-care also involves knowing your limits and not overcommitting. It's okay to say no to additional tasks if they will compromise your ability to perform effectively. Prioritizing and reassigning tasks can help manage workload more efficiently, reducing the risk of burnout. Remember, taking care of yourself enables you to contribute more effectively in the long run.

Addressing misunderstandings and conflicts is essential for maintaining a positive work environment. Misunderstandings are common in any workplace but can be particularly challenging for neurodiverse individuals. When disputes arise, addressing them calmly and promptly can prevent escalation and foster a culture of openness and resolution.

Start by drilling down the root cause of the misunderstanding. Was there a miscommunication? Different expectations? Once identified, approach the concerned party with a mindset geared towards finding a solution, not assigning blame. Using non-confrontational language and active listening can ease tensions. Phrases like "I noticed that..." or "I feel..." can open up dialogue without sounding accusatory (Hopler, W., 2022).

Conflict resolution also benefits from predefined strategies. A standard procedure for handling disputes ensures everyone knows what steps to follow, making the process less daunting. This could involve meeting with a mediator or HR representative to facilitate discussions, ensuring a fair and unbiased resolution.

Regular feedback sessions can prevent many misunderstandings. Encouraging a culture where feedback is given constructively and received openly helps address issues before they become significant problems. It creates an atmosphere where continuous improvement is valued, and everyone feels heard and respected.

Balancing Professional Responsibilities with Unmasking and Self-Discovery

Balancing the demands of professional duties with the journey of unmasking and self-discovery is no simple feat, especially for late-diagnosed autistic adults and individuals with ADHD. However, setting realistic goals and priorities can create a structure accommodating work tasks and personal development. This involves recognizing limitations and strengths and allocating time and energy accordingly. A practical approach might be breaking down larger projects into smaller, manageable tasks, allowing for occasional reassessment and adjustment of goals based on current circumstances.

Realistic goal-setting also means being honest about what can be achieved within given timeframes without compromising well-being. For instance, it is crucial to balance attending to job duties and engaging in activities that foster self-discovery, such as joining support groups or pursuing hobbies. Moreover, tools like planners or digital apps to track progress can help keep priorities in check, ensuring that professional and personal growth is addressed.

Another aspect of this balancing act is communicating needs effectively to colleagues and supervisors. Expressing the need for flexible schedules or specific working conditions in precise terms can pave the way for understanding and support in the workplace. By creating an open dialogue, individuals can foster an environment where their professional responsibilities are met while dedicating time to personal growth endeavors.

Identifying areas for growth and skill development is another essential part of navigating the professional landscape. For career advancement, it's beneficial to first recognize one's current skill set and then determine the gaps that need bridging. This might involve seeking feedback from peers or mentors who can provide insights into areas requiring improvement. Regular self-assessment exercises can also help pinpoint strengths and weaknesses, guiding future learning efforts.

Pursuing opportunities for training and professional development can significantly impact career trajectories. Enrolling in workshops, online courses, or certification programs aligns personal interests with professional requirements. Many companies also offer internal training modules tailored to equip employees with new skills. Actively participating in such initiatives enhances competence and demonstrates a commitment to self-improvement—an attractive trait in any professional setting.

It's important to remember that career development is a continuous journey. Embracing a mindset focused on lifelong learning ensures that individuals remain adaptable and prepared for evolving job markets. This proactive personal and skill development approach lays a stronger foundation for achieving long-term career goals.

Embracing authentic self-expression in professional interactions is critical to fostering genuine connections.

Authenticity allows individuals to present themselves truthfully, which can lead to increasingly meaningful and productive relationships at work. By aligning actions and communications with one's true self, trust and respect are established among colleagues. This authenticity can also serve as a catalyst for creativity and innovation, encouraging diverse perspectives in problem-solving.

However, embracing authenticity requires a conscious effort to unmask. This involves slowly revealing one's true nature, preferences, and behaviors that may have been previously concealed to conform to workplace norms. It can start with small steps, such as sharing personal interests or opinions during meetings. Over time, these efforts build confidence in one's identity, paving the way for fuller self-expression.

Creating a supportive network is also vital for maintaining authenticity. Connecting with like-minded colleagues or joining employee resource groups dedicated to neurodiversity can provide a safe space for sharing experiences and challenges. These networks not only amplify the voices of neurodiverse individuals but also advocate for inclusive practices within the organization, promoting a culture where everyone feels valued and understood.

Recognizing the importance of self-awareness and self-compassion in maintaining healthy boundaries cannot be overstated. Self-awareness involves understanding one's emotional triggers, strengths, and areas needing improvement. This insight helps individuals navigate professional settings more productively and make informed decisions aligned with their values. According to Tasha Eurich, only 15% of people are self-aware, highlighting its rarity and value (The Path of Self-

Awareness in the Workplace: Embracing Your Authentic Self - Galt Foundation., 2023).

On the other hand, practicing self-compassion entails treating oneself with kindness and patience, particularly when facing setbacks. It means acknowledging that mistakes and challenges are part of the human experience and refraining from harsh self-criticism. This attitude fosters resilience, enabling individuals to bounce back from difficulties and maintain their well-being. Mindfulness techniques, including meditation or journaling, can enhance self-awareness and cultivate a compassionate outlook.

Setting boundaries is a practical application of self-awareness and self-compassion. Clear boundaries between work and personal life protect one's authenticity and prevent burnout. This might involve setting specific work hours, taking regular breaks, or carving out time for activities that bring joy and relaxation. Communicating these boundaries to colleagues ensures mutual respect and understanding, allowing for a healthier work-life balance.

Showcasing Success Stories and Promoting a Culture of Inclusion

In today's professional world, the importance of unmasking and embracing authenticity cannot be overstated, especially for late-diagnosed autistic adults and individuals with ADHD. Highlighting real-world examples of workplace unmasking celebrates achievements and inspires others facing similar challenges. For instance, Alex Sobil, a Cybersecurity Analyst at Dell Technologies, successfully navigated his career by joining a neurodiversity hiring program which provided him with the necessary accommodations and support (Neurodiversity Community Self-Advocate, Writer, Author, and Public Speaker Archives. Autism Spectrum News., n.d.). Sharing such stories reinforces the idea that unmasking can lead to remarkable personal and professional milestones.

Celebrating these achievements also underscores the resilience and strength of neurodivergent individuals. Kaelynn Partlow, a therapist and dog trainer, found success as a star on the Netflix series "Love on the Spectrum" by openly embracing her identity. Her journey is a beacon of hope, illustrating that authenticity can pave the way for broader acceptance and representation. Through narratives like hers, we learn that breaking free from societal expectations is possible and rewarding.

Encouraging organizations to embrace neurodiversity through inclusive hiring practices is vital for creating supportive work environments. Inclusive hiring begins with recognizing that standard recruitment methods often overlook the unique strengths and capabilities of neurodivergent individuals. Companies like Dell Technologies have set a precedent by adjusting their hiring processes to better accommodate neurodiverse candidates. This includes modifying interview formats to reduce anxiety and focusing on practical assessments highlighting candidates' skills.

Implementing neurodiversity-friendly policies requires a commitment to ongoing education and training within organizations. By fostering awareness and understanding, employers can create an atmosphere where all employees feel appreciated and supported. Leaders must advocate for these changes and ensure that neurodiverse employees are provided equal opportunities to thrive. This approach not only enhances diversity but also improves overall organizational performance.

Allowing for a culture of respect and understanding for individual differences in professional environments goes beyond inclusive hiring practices. It involves creating workplaces where employees can openly express themselves without the anxiety of judgment or discrimination. Open dialogues about neurodiversity help break down misconceptions and build empathy among colleagues. When team members understand each other's unique perspectives and needs, they can collaborate more effectively and support one another better.

Organizations can promote this culture by implementing mentorship programs, peer support groups, and regular training sessions on neurodiversity. These initiatives encourage open communication and create safe environments for employees to discuss their experiences and challenges. By constructing a foundation of mutual respect and understanding, companies can create inclusive environments where everyone feels accepted and valued.

Engaging in advocacy efforts and connecting with communities that promote neurodiversity awareness play crucial roles in driving societal change. Advocacy can include public speaking engagements, writing articles, and sharing personal stories online. By increasing awareness and examining the importance of neurodiverse inclusion, advocates help shift public perceptions and reduce stigma.

Connecting with broader neurodiverse online and offline communities provides valuable support and resources for individuals navigating their professional journeys. These networks offer a sense of solidarity and empowerment, reminding neurodivergent individuals that they are not alone in their experiences. These communities can drive policy changes through collective advocacy and promote greater acceptance in workplaces and beyond.

Promoting neurodiversity awareness also involves collaborating with other organizations and stakeholders. Engaging with policymakers, educators, and industry leaders helps amplify the message and ensures that neurodiversity is recognized and prioritized across various sectors. Working together can produce a more inclusive community where everyone can succeed.

Navigating Workplace Realities while Embracing Authenticity

Understanding legal rights and workplace accommodations is a crucial component in the journey toward unmasking and embracing authenticity for late-diagnosed autistic adults and individuals with ADHD. The ADA offers protection against discrimination and ensures reasonable accommodations, fostering an environment where neurodiverse individuals can thrive professionally. Requests for these accommodations require clear communication and sometimes documentation from healthcare providers. By knowing their rights and advocating for themselves, neurodiverse employees can create a work environment tailored to their needs.

It is crucial to recognize and address workplace discrimination. Companies have policies and procedures in place, but understanding these and being prepared to document and report instances of discrimination can empower individuals to stand up for their rights. It's about modifying physical spaces and nurturing a culture of acceptance and inclusivity. This includes educating peers and promoting understanding to reduce stigma and foster empathy.

Another significant consideration is whether to disclose one's neurodivergence at work. Disclosure can lead to better support and accommodations but comes with potential bias or judgment risks. People must weigh these factors thoughtfully to make the best decision for themselves.

Communication skills are pivotal in expressing needs and fostering workplace inclusion. Practicing assertive communication, using "I" statements, and preparing for conversations are effective strategies. Assertive communication helps articulate needs and set boundaries, reducing misunderstandings and stress. Building solid relationships with colleagues and mentors further supports a positive work environment. These connections provide a supportive network, offering insights and encouragement necessary for professional success.

Self-care and managing stress are vital. Regular breaks, mindfulness exercises, and suitable work environments help maintain well-being. Communicating self-care needs to the team ensures understanding and cooperation, enabling productivity without compromising health. Recognizing one's limits and prioritizing tasks prevents overcommitment and burnout, making balancing professional responsibilities and personal growth easier.

Addressing misunderstandings and conflicts can maintain a harmonious work environment. Identifying the root cause of disputes and approaching them fosters resolution and openness. Regular feedback sessions preempt many issues, creating a culture of continuous improvement where everyone feels heard.

Balancing professional responsibilities with unmasking and self-discovery involves setting realistic goals and priorities. Breaking down more significant assignments into manageable tasks and utilizing tools like planners helps keep track of progress. Effective communication with colleagues about flexible schedules and working conditions fosters support. Pursuing training and professional development opportunities aligns personal interests with career advancement, ensuring continuous skill growth.

Embracing authentic self-expression strengthens workplace connections. Authenticity nurtures trust and respect among colleagues and fuels creativity and innovation. Gradually revealing preferences and behaviors builds confidence, facilitating fuller self-expression over time. Creating a supportive network, joining employee resource groups, and practicing self-compassion and self-awareness are essential in navigating professional settings effectively.

Showcasing success stories and promoting a culture of inclusion highlights the achievements of neurodiverse individuals and inspires others. Celebrating these stories underscores resilience and strength, and demonstrating authenticity leads to remarkable milestones. Encouraging inclusive hiring practices and implementing neurodiversity-friendly policies enhance organizational performance and foster supportive environments. Advocacy efforts and connecting with communities promote greater awareness, driving societal change.

In reflecting on these strategies, remember that unmasking and embracing authenticity is a unique journey for each individual. The path may be challenging, but with suitable support systems, neurodiverse individuals can thrive while staying true to themselves. As we continue to promote understanding and inclusivity, we pave the way for a more diverse and accepting world.

Ongoing Journey: Embracing Lifelong Growth and Change

E mbracing lifelong growth and change is a dynamic process with opportunities for self-discovery and adaptation. For late-diagnosed autistic adults and individuals with ADHD, this journey involves uncovering the layers of behaviors adopted to blend in with societal norms, known as masking. Shedding these masks offers a chance to connect deeply with one's true self and live more authentically. Through ongoing introspection and reflection, you begin to unravel the patterns shaped by external pressures and recognize the genuine desires that define your unique identity.

This chapter will explore how cultivating self-awareness is essential for maintaining authenticity while navigating continuous growth and change. Let's dive into strategies for acknowledging strengths and weaknesses, fostering personal acceptance, and setting realistic goals aligned with your true self. Additionally, we'll discuss the importance of staying open to change and developing adaptability and resilience in the face of life's unpredictability. The insights shared will assist with understanding the value of aligning your actions with core values, enabling a harmonious and fulfilling life journey toward ongoing development and self-discovery.

Developing lifelong strategies for maintaining authenticity

As we embark on the ongoing journey of embracing lifelong growth and change, developing strategies for maintaining authenticity is crucial. For late-diagnosed autistic adults and individuals with ADHD, understanding and unmasking behaviors play a significant role in connecting with their true selves. Cultivating self-awareness is the first step toward this goal. Understanding oneself involves continuous introspection and self-reflection. Taking time to examine your thoughts, emotions, and actions allows you to recognize patterns that may have been influenced by external expectations rather than your genuine desires. Regularly engaging in self-reflection can identify areas where you may have been masking or conforming to societal norms and begin the unmasking process.

Acknowledging your strengths and weaknesses is vital for personal growth. Embracing both aspects of yourself allows for a balanced view of your capabilities and areas for improvement. Celebrating your strengths boosts self-confidence while recognizing your weaknesses provides growth opportunities. This honest assessment helps you understand what makes you unique and enables you to set realistic goals that align with your authentic self. By focusing on personal growth rather than comparison with others, you cultivate a sense of self-acceptance and authenticity.

Being open to change and uncertainty fosters adaptability and resilience. Life is brimming with unpredictable moments, and learning to navigate these changes without losing your sense of self is essential. Letting go of rigid expectations about how things should be allows for personal evolution. Embracing adaptation as an opportunity for growth rather than a threat encourages a positive mindset. This adaptability enhances your ability to cope with life's challenges and opens doors to new experiences and perspectives contributing to your ongoing development.

Staying true to your core values is fundamental to maintaining authenticity. Your values are the guiding principles that form your decisions and actions. Consistently aligning your behavior with these values reinforces your sense of self-integrity. Reflecting on your core values can provide clarity and direction when faced with difficult choices or external pressures. This alignment between your actions and beliefs fosters a deep sense of authenticity and fulfillment. Knowing that you live according to your principles builds self-trust and confidence in your decisions.

Aligning your actions with your values enhances self-integrity and authenticity. It is easy to be swayed by the opinions and expectations of others, but staying true to your values requires courage and conviction. By making conscious choices that reflect your beliefs, you create a life that is genuinely your own. This alignment brings a sense of harmony and purpose, as your actions represent who you are. Additionally, it strengthens your relationships with others, as they see your authenticity and are more likely to trust and respect you.

Navigating challenges while staying true to yourself fosters emotional well-being. Life's obstacles can sometimes push you to act in ways inconsistent with your values. However, remaining authentic in the face of adversity contributes to emotional resilience. It ensures you keep sight of your true self, even in challenging circumstances. This resilience is built through practice and reflection, helping you to maintain your integrity and emotional health over time. By staying true to yourself, you navigate life's ebbs and flows with a grounded sense of identity and purpose.

Adapting to new life stages and challenges

Adapting to new life stages and challenges can be a transformative process. It's essential to understand that transitioning between different phases in life requires both flexibility and a growth mindset. For late-diagnosed autistic adults and individuals with ADHD, this can mean unlearning old patterns of behavior that were used to mask their true selves. Embracing authenticity allows for a fuller expression of who they are, making transitions less daunting.

It's crucial to remain open-minded and adaptable. Situations will change, and this includes how we approach them. For example, moving from the structure of a school environment into the workforce involves shifting daily routines and expectations. Developing a flexible attitude helps adjust to these new circumstances and can mitigate the stress of change.

Moreover, adopting a growth mindset enables individuals to see challenges not as obstacles but as opportunities for personal development. When faced with a new life stage, whether starting a new job, entering a new relationship, or even aging, viewing these changes as chances to grow fosters resilience. It's about understanding that each phase has something to teach us, helping us to better navigate future transitions.

Embracing new roles and responsibilities is another critical aspect of adapting to life's challenges. As we move through different stages, our roles evolve, and so do our responsibilities. For someone diagnosed later in life with autism or ADHD, this might mean re-evaluating their role in their family or workplace. Understanding and accepting these new expectations opens avenues for personal and professional growth.

It's beneficial to approach new responsibilities with curiosity and openness. For instance, becoming a parent introduces many new tasks and responsibilities. Viewing these challenges through a lens of growth can make the metamorphosis smoother and more fulfilling. Each responsibility contributes to personal development and building skills and strengths previously untapped.

Guidelines can be beneficial in this context. Setting clear goals and objectives when stepping into a new role can provide direction and focus. It may also be helpful to seek mentorship from those who have successfully navigated similar transitions. Learning from their wisdom can offer practical advice and support, making the journey more manageable.

Overcoming obstacles with resilience and problem-solving skills is crucial for personal growth. Life inevitably presents challenges, some expected and others unforeseen. Resilience is the ability to bounce back from these difficulties, while problem-solving skills equip individuals to tackle them head-on. For late-diagnosed autistic adults and individuals with ADHD, these skills can be especially vital in managing the unique challenges they face.

Resilience can be built by adopting an optimistic viewpoint and focusing on what can be controlled. When challenges arise, breaking them down into manageable pieces makes them feel less overwhelming. For example, if someone struggles with social interactions at a new job, they can set small, achievable goals, like daily initiating a conversation with one colleague. Over time, these small steps build confidence and resilience.

Furthermore, developing solid problem-solving skills enhances one's ability to cope with challenges. This involves identifying the problem, brainstorming possible solutions, evaluating the options, and selecting the best course of action. Seeking input from trusted friends, family, or professionals can also provide additional perspectives and solutions, making it easier to overcome obstacles.

Viewing barriers as opportunities for learning and growth shifts perspective. Instead of seeing setbacks as failures, they should be considered valuable learning experiences. This change in mindset can reduce anxiety and promote a more proactive approach to challenges. For example, if a project at work doesn't go as planned, reflecting on what went wrong and how to improve next time turns the experience into a growth opportunity rather than a dead end.

Seeking support from others during challenging times fosters emotional resilience. No one has to face challenges alone; reaching out for help can provide much-needed emotional support and practical advice. For individuals with ADHD or autism, finding a community or support group where they feel understood and accepted can be incredibly empowering. Sharing approaches and strategies with others who face similar challenges can dull feelings of isolation and reinforce a sense of belonging.

Professional help, such as therapy or coaching, can also be invaluable. Mental health professionals provide methods and techniques to manage stress, anxiety, and other emotional reactions to life's challenges. They can offer personalized advice that accounts for the unique needs of late-diagnosed autistic adults and individuals with ADHD, creating a supportive environment where personal growth is nurtured.

Embracing change as a catalyst for growth encourages self-evolution. Change is an inevitable part of life, and how we respond to it shapes our growth and development. Individuals can develop a more resilient and adaptive mindset by welcoming change and viewing it as a chance to evolve. This perspective can be remarkably liberating for those who have spent years masking their true selves. Embracing their authentic identity becomes an integral part of their ongoing journey.

Recognizing that change is a natural part of life reduces resistance and anxiety. Accepting that change is constant makes us more comfortable with uncertainty. This acceptance can alleviate fears associated with the unknown for someone navigating a new diagnosis or life stage. It allows them to focus on the present moment and adapt to changes as they come rather than being paralyzed by what might happen.

Continued learning and personal development

Understanding and embracing a lifelong learning mindset is crucial for personal development. This approach means constantly striving to acquire new knowledge and skills, which can profoundly impact one's life. For late-diagnosed autistic adults and individuals with ADHD, this journey might be more complicated due to unique challenges, but the benefits of continuous learning are immense. By committing to a lifelong learning mindset, you open yourself to new opportunities and growth, fostering a sense of achievement and self-empowerment.

Setting personal growth goals is another essential component of continued learning and personal development. Establishing clear and attainable goals provides a roadmap for progress and keeps you motivated. When setting these goals, it's helpful to break them into smaller, manageable steps. This makes the goals seem less daunting and creates a structure that helps track your progress. Celebrating small milestones can boost your confidence and motivation, propelling you further.

Exploring personal development resources such as books, workshops, and mentors supports your growth. These resources offer precious insights and practical tips that can guide you on your path. For instance, reading books on topics of interest can expand your knowledge base, while attending workshops can provide hands-on experience and networking opportunities. Connecting with mentors who have walked similar paths can offer guidance, support, and inspiration.

Networking with like-minded individuals is another powerful tool in your personal development arsenal. Engaging with a community of people who share your interests and challenges creates a support system where you can trade ideas, seek advice, and collaborate on projects. This sense of community fosters a collaborative environment that encourages growth and learning from each other's experiences. These connections can be indispensable in your journey through in-person meetings or online forums.

Embracing curiosity and intellectual growth leads to personal transformation. Being curious involves asking questions, exploring new ideas, and challenging assumptions. This mindset nurtures intellectual growth, enabling you to see the world from different perspectives and adapt to new situations more effectively. Intellectual curiosity fuels creativity and problem-solving skills, making it easier to navigate life's complexities.

Continuing to seek knowledge and new experiences broadens your perspectives and enhances your skills. Engaging in activities outside your comfort zone pushes you to expand your abilities and adapt to new circumstances. Whether learning a new language, trying a new hobby, or traveling to unfamiliar locations, these experiences enrich your life and contribute to personal growth. They also help build resilience and adaptability, essential traits for managing change.

Setting personal growth goals also involves regular self-reflection and evaluation. Taking time to reflect on your achievements and areas for improvement helps align your goals with your values and aspirations. This practice ensures that your growth is meaningful and aligned with your true self.

Regularly revisiting and adjusting your goals based on your evolving needs and circumstances keeps you on track and motivated.

Investing time in self-improvement activities enhances overall well-being and fulfillment. Mindfulness, exercise, and hobbies contribute to your mental and physical health, creating a balanced and satisfying life. Self-improvement goes beyond professional development; it encompasses all areas of life, including relationships, health, and personal passions. Prioritizing these activities ensures a holistic approach to personal growth, leading to a more fulfilling life.

Seeking personal development resources tailored to your needs can significantly impact your journey. For late-diagnosed autistic adults and individuals with ADHD, finding resources that address specific challenges and strengths can be particularly beneficial. Books, online courses, and support groups designed for neurodivergent individuals offer targeted strategies and insights that resonate with your experiences, making them more effective.

Networking within specialized communities can provide additional support and understanding. Engaging with others with similar experiences creates a safe space for exchanging ideas and offering mutual support. These connections can be particularly empowering, as they validate your experiences and provide encouragement. Collaborative projects and shared goals within these communities can lead to unparalleled personal and collective growth.

Finally, maintaining a commitment to continuous learning and personal development requires resilience and perseverance. The journey is not always easy, and setbacks are inevitable.

However, viewing these challenges as opportunities for learning and growth can transform obstacles into stepping stones. Staying adaptable and open-minded enables you to navigate changes more smoothly, turning each experience into a valuable lesson.

Fostering resilience and self-confidence through ongoing change

Fostering resilience and self-confidence through ongoing change is crucial for late-diagnosed autistic adults and individuals with ADHD. Navigating life's unpredictabilities requires a robust emotional toolkit. One essential tool is cultivating resilience, which provides the ability to recover from setbacks and face challenges head-on.

Building resilience starts with developing coping strategies and support systems. Establishing a network of friends, family, and professionals who understand and offer encouragement creates a safety net during tough times. Through trial and error, discovering what personally works best helps manage stress and reduces the likelihood of feeling overwhelmed. Techniques such as mindfulness, regular exercise, and hobbies bring about balance and aid in maintaining mental well-being.

Another aspect of resilience is viewing failures as learning opportunities. Reframing mistakes can transform what could be debilitating into valuable lessons. This perspective shift bolsters emotional strength and adaptability. Every setback becomes an experience that teaches essential skills and insights, fostering a proactive and optimistic outlook on life.

Nurturing self-confidence involves embracing one's strengths and abilities. Understanding personal talents and celebrating achievements, no matter how small builds a foundation of self-belief. Recognizing these qualities shifts focus from perceived shortcomings to areas of competence and growth. Celebrating progress reinforces positive self-perception and encourages continued effort.

Positive self-talk and self-affirmations boost self-esteem and self-assurance. Repeating affirming statements can counteract negative thoughts and cultivate a more confident mindset. These affirmations remind individuals of their worth and potential, creating a more resilient self-image. Small yet consistent practices like this gradually build a stronger sense of self.

Stepping out of your comfort zone is another effective way to foster self-confidence and promote personal growth. Challenging oneself with new experiences and tasks encourages the development of new abilities and coping mechanisms. Each successful venture enhances self-efficacy, making future challenges more manageable and less intimidating.

Embracing self-compassion during times of change and challenge reduces self-criticism and anxiety. Treating oneself with kindness and understanding mirrors the empathy extended to others. Acknowledging that everyone's struggles and imperfections are part of the human experience helps mitigate harsh self-judgments. This practice encourages a healthier relationship with oneself.

Treating oneself with kindness and understanding promotes emotional resilience. It allows individuals to recover more readily from setbacks by reducing the intensity of negative emotions. Self-compassion involves accepting that struggling does not equate to failure but indicates an ongoing growth journey. By fostering an empathetic inner dialogue, individuals can navigate difficulties without amplifying feelings of inadequacy or despair.

Finally, embracing imperfections and mistakes as part of the growth process fosters self-acceptance. Accepting that nobody is perfect liberates individuals from unrealistic expectations and constant self-reproach. This acceptance nurtures a more compassionate and forgiving attitude towards oneself, allowing for more excellent emotional stability and resilience when faced with new challenges.

Emphasizing the need for self-awareness, adaptability, continuous learning, and resilience in embracing lifelong growth and change.

Throughout this chapter, we have explored the importance of continuous self-growth and how it intertwines with maintaining authenticity. We've discussed the necessity of understanding oneself through introspection and self-reflection, identifying patterns that might influence societal expectations, and beginning the process of unmasking behaviors. For late-diagnosed autistic adults and individuals with ADHD, this self-awareness is a vital step toward embracing authentic living.

Reflecting on our unique strengths and weaknesses has also been highlighted as crucial for personal growth. By acknowledging both aspects, we can set realistic goals that align with our authentic selves, fostering self-acceptance and authenticity. This honest assessment helps build a balanced view of our capabilities and areas for improvement, ultimately enhancing self-confidence.

Staying open to change and uncertainty plays a significant role in cultivating adaptability and resilience. Life's unpredictable nature requires us to let go of rigid expectations and embrace change as an opportunity for growth. This perspective helps us cope with challenges and opens up new experiences and perspectives, contributing to our ongoing development.

Staying true to our core values has emerged as a foundation for maintaining authenticity. Our values guide our decisions and actions, reinforcing a sense of self-integrity. When faced with challenging decisions or external pressures, reflecting on these values provides clarity and direction, fostering a sense of fulfillment and authenticity.

Moreover, aligning actions with values enhances emotional well-being and strengthens relationships. By making conscious choices that reflect our beliefs, we create a life that genuinely represents who we are. This alignment brings harmony and purpose and invites trust and respect from others, deepening our connections.

Navigating life's difficulties while staying true to oneself contributes significantly to emotional resilience. Life's obstacles can test our values, but remaining authentic in adversity ensures we do not lose sight of our true selves. This resilience is built through practice and reflection, helping us maintain integrity and emotional health.

Adapting to new life stages and overcoming obstacles with resilience and problem-solving skills were also essential points covered. Embracing new roles and responsibilities with curiosity and openness allows for personal and professional growth. Setting clear goals and seeking mentorship can provide direction during transitions, making them less daunting.

Resilience and problem-solving skills equip individuals to tackle life's challenges head-on. Perceiving setbacks as learning opportunities rather than failures promotes a proactive approach to difficulties. Additionally, seeking support from others fosters emotional resilience, diminishing feelings of isolation and reinforcing a sense of belonging.

Continued learning and personal development remain critical for lifelong growth. Embracing a lifelong learning mindset, setting personal growth goals, and exploring various resources empower individuals to acquire new knowledge and skills. Networking with like-minded individuals and engaging in activities outside one's comfort zone further enriches personal development.

Lastly, fostering resilience and self-confidence through ongoing change involves developing coping strategies and support systems. Viewing failures as learning opportunities and nurturing self-confidence by embracing strengths and abilities are crucial steps. Positive self-talk, stepping out of comfort zones, and practicing self-compassion during times of change all contribute to building a more resilient and confident self.

As we move forward, it's important to remember that the journey of self-growth and adaptation is ongoing. Embracing change and maintaining authenticity requires continuous effort and reflection. Each phase of life presents new challenges and opportunities, offering valuable lessons that contribute to our evolution. Let us remain committed to this path, navigating life's unpredictabilities with resilience and confidence while staying true to our authentic selves. The journey may be arduous but immensely rewarding, leading to a life of greater fulfillment and self-discovery.

Conclusion

As you close this chapter of your journey, it's imperative to take a moment to reflect on where you've been and where you're headed. This book has aimed to be more than just a collection of words and stories; it's intended to be a companion for those diagnosed with autism or ADHD, guiding you through the intricate journey of unmasking and embracing your true self.

You have absorbed various experiences and strategies throughout these pages, each designed to help you reconnect with who you genuinely are. Perhaps you found resonance in the shared stories that mirrored your struggles, triumphs, and the delicate process of peeling away layers of societal masks to reveal your inner child. Remember, every step you take toward embracing authenticity is a significant milestone in your personal development. The path may be winding and unpredictable, but it is uniquely yours—a testament to your resilience and courage.

As you navigate this labyrinth of self-discovery, embracing vulnerability becomes crucial. It may seem paradoxical, but there is profound strength in allowing yourself to be seen as you are. Vulnerability is not a sign of weakness but rather an act of profound bravery. Consider the metaphor of a seedling breaking through the soil, striving toward sunlight. It's fragile but remarkably determined, driven by an innate potential to flourish. In much the same way, your authenticity yearns to break free and blossom. Exposing your true self allows others to see the beauty of your uniqueness and pave the way for deeper, more meaningful connections.

Another cornerstone of your journey should be self-compassion. Unmasking is not a linear process; it's fraught with highs and lows, moments of clarity and confusion. During these fluctuations, treating yourself with kindness and understanding is crucial. Imagine how you would support a dear friend going through a similar experience—offering them words of encouragement, a listening ear, and forgiveness when they stumble. Now, extend that same grace to yourself. Celebrate small victories, no matter how minor, because each signifies forward momentum. Acknowledge the labor and courage it takes to confront deeply ingrained behaviors and beliefs.

Growth is an ongoing process, and it doesn't end with the last page of this book. Your journey towards embracing your inner child and living authentically continues beyond these words. Seek out communities that foster acceptance and understanding. Surround yourself with individuals who celebrate your progress and provide the emotional scaffolding needed to navigate challenges. These supportive networks can offer invaluable insights, shared wisdom, and a sense of belonging that strengthens your resolve to remain authentic.

Remaining open to new possibilities is equally essential. Just as life is dynamic, so too is your journey of self-discovery. Be receptive to change and new experiences that might illuminate different facets of your identity. Maintain a curious and flexible mindset, recognizing that your understanding of yourself will evolve. The journey toward authenticity has no final destination; it is an ever-expanding horizon filled with opportunities for growth and enlightenment.

Through unmasking, you unlock the richness of living as your genuine self. You may find that embracing authenticity leads to profound internal transformations—shifts in perspectives, altered priorities, and newfound passions. However, it's also likely to bring about external changes: deeper relationships, more fulfilling endeavors, and a sense of alignment between your inner world and outer actions.

Throughout this book, you have encountered various tools and techniques to dismantle the masks you wear. Each technique serves as a stepping stone to self-acceptance, from mindfulness practices to creative outlets, from introspective exercises to community engagement. Keep these strategies close to your heart, revisiting them as necessary. They are not one-time fixes but lifelong companions that will assist you in navigating future challenges.

Remember that while unmasking might initially feel like a solitary endeavor, you are not alone. Many have walked this path before you, and many will follow. Your courage contributes to a growing collective consciousness that values authenticity over conformity. Living true to oneself inspires others to do the same, creating a ripple effect that fosters a more inclusive and empathetic world.

In conclusion, cherish the lessons learned and the growth achieved as you move forward. Honor your journey with all its complexities and nuances. Whether tentative or bold, each step brings you closer to a more authentic existence. Embrace your vulnerabilities, practice steadfast self-compassion, seek continuous growth, and remain open to new horizons. Your inner child awaits, eager to explore the world with fresh eyes and an open heart.

Your path toward unmasking and authenticity is yours alone, but it is interwoven with the journeys of countless others. We form a tapestry of resilience, courage, and genuine connection. So, take a deep breath, hold your head high, and enter the fullness of who you are. The journey of unmasking is not just a destination but a way of being—a continuous dance with the essence of your true self. As you progress, you may find joy, peace, and unwavering confidence in your journey.

Dear Reader,

Thank you for reading my book on unmasking late-diagnosed autism. I hope it has not only provided valuable insights but also been a supportive companion on your unique journey.

If you found the book helpful, I would appreciate it if you took a moment to write a review. Your feedback is incredibly important and helps other readers discover my book.

Thank you for your support!

Warm regards,

Hillary Sartor

References

C haper 1

Begeer, S., Kentrou, V., Mataw, K., de Veld, D. (2018, September). *Delayed autism spectrum disorder recognition in children and adolescents previously diagnosed with attention-deficit/hyperactivity disorder. Autism.* None

Hill, D. (2020, June). *From the Frontlines: The Truth About Masks and COVID-19 | American Lung Association. www.lung.org.* https://www.lung.org/blog/covid-masks

Link to external site, t. (2023, September). *The workplace masking experiences of autistic, non-autistic neurodivergent and neurotypical adults in the UK. ProQuest.* https://www.proquest.com/docview/2861634558/ECA612CE5251437APQ/5?accountid=12372

Miller, D., Pearson, A., Rees, J. (2021, May). *"Masking is life": Experiences of masking in autistic and nonautistic adults. Autism in Adulthood.* https://www.liebertpub.com/doi/abs/10.1089/aut.2020.0083

Nyce, J., Timpka, T. (2021, April). *Face mask use during the Covid-19 pandemic – the significance of culture and the symbolic meaning of behaviour. Annals of Epidemiology.* None

Chapter 2

55+ Self-Discovery Questions for Personal Growth [+ Printables]. University of St. Augustine for Health Sciences. (2020, April). https://www.usa.edu/blog/self-discovery-questions/

Anonymous. (2023). *A Late Diagnosis, Questions Answered, and Self-Acceptance* . *AANE* . Retrieved from https://aane.org/autism-info-faqs/library/a-late-diagnosis-questions-answered-and-self-acceptance/

Brewer, R., Cage, E., Corden, K. (2021, July). *Personal Identity After an Autism Diagnosis: Relationships With Self-Esteem, Mental Wellbeing, and Diagnostic Timing. Frontiers in Psychology.* None

Fairbank, R. (2023). *An ADHD diagnosis in adulthood comes with challenges and benefits. Apa.org.* https://www.apa.org/monitor/2023/03/adult-adhd-diagnosis

Ghanouni, P., Quirke, S. (2022, January). *Resilience and Coping Strategies in Adults with Autism Spectrum Disorder. Journal of Autism and Developmental Disorders.* None

LeBoeuf, R. (2022, June). *50 Best Personal Growth Quotes. Southern New Hampshire University.* https://www.snhu.edu/about-us/newsroom/education/personal-growth-quotes

Chapter 3

Bahns, A., Crandall, C., Gillath, O. (2022, September). *Do masks affect social interaction?. Journal of Applied Social Psychology.* None

Chen, C., Feng, Z., Ma, Q., Shi, S., Wang, Y., Wu, Y., Yang, Q., Yao, Y., Yuan, X., Zhang, K., Zhang, Y. (2024, March). *Effect of*

Surgical Masks and N95 Respirators on Anxiety. Neuropsychiatric disease and treatment. https:// www.ncbi.nlm.nih.gov/pmc/articles/PMC10933521/ #:~:text=One%20study%20found%20that%20wearing

Czeisler, C., Czeisler, M., Howard, M., Lane, R., Rajaratnam, S., Wolkow, A. (2023, March). *Association between burnout and adherence with mask usage and additional COVID-19 prevention behaviours: findings from a large-scale, demographically representative survey of US adults. BMJ Open.* None

Ding, S., Xia, T., Xu, X. (2023, November). *A study of the relationship between social anxiety and mask-wearing intention among college students in the post-COVID-19 era: mediating effects of self-identity, impression management, and avoidance. Frontiers in Psychology.* None

Fan, K., Lin, H., Liu, P., Lou, X., Mao, Z., Wang, C., Wang, J., Wang, X., Wei, D., Wu, C., Xu, Q. (2022, February). *Association between mask wearing and anxiety symptoms during the outbreak of COVID 19: A large survey among 386,432 junior and senior high school students in China. Journal of Psychosomatic Research.* https:// www.sciencedirect.com/science/article/pii/ S0022399921003548

Herrera-Peco, I., Jurado, M., Linares, J., Martín, A., Martínez, Á., Pérez-Fuentes, M. (2022, August). *The "Mask Effect" of the Emotional Factor in Nurses' Adaptability to Change: Mental Health in a COVID-19 Setting. Healthcare.* https://doaj.org/ article/356b4f1749a0434da833b41f92ce1993

Villani, C., D'Ascenzo, S., Scerrati, E., Ricciardelli, P., Nicoletti, R., & Lugli, L. (2022). *Wearing the face mask affects our* social attention over space . *Frontiers in Psychology* , 13. https://doi.org/10.3389/fpsyg.2022.923558

Chapter 4

MindTools | Home. www.mindtools.com. (n.d.). https://www.riverland.edu/student-services/study-skills/goals-and-goal-setting/

Success, T. (n.d.). *Goal Setting Techniques: Ways To Effectively Set and Achieve Goals. www.nsls.org.* https://www.nsls.org/goal-setting-techniques

Chapter 5

Bethany, H., Senko, K. (2019). *PLAY THERAPY: An Illustrative Case. Innovations in Clinical Neuroscience.* https://www.ncbi.nlm.nih.gov/pmc/articles/PMC6659989/

Hestbech, A. (2018, July). *Reclaiming the Inner Child in Cognitive-Behavioral Therapy: The Complementary Model of the Personality. American Journal of Psychotherapy.* None

*How Memories of Childhood Trauma Affect Us Today | CPTSDfoundation.org. * (n.d.). https://cptsdfoundation.org/2024/01/29/how-memories-of-childhood-trauma-affect-us-today/

Kostenius, C., Prellwitz, M., Sjöblom, M., Öhrling, K. (2016, January). *Health throughout the lifespan: The phenomenon of the inner child reflected in events during childhood experienced by older persons. International Journal of Qualitative Studies on Health and Well-being.* None

Self-compassion practices. Self-Compassion. (n.d.). https://self-compassion.org/self-compassion-practices/

Therapy Services - Clear Minds. https://clearminds.ca/therapy-services/

Trauma-Focused Therapy Techniques. concept.paloaltou.edu. (n.d.). https://concept.paloaltou.edu/resources/business-of-practice-blog/trauma-focused-therapy-techniques

What are Somatic Therapy Exercises for Healing Trauma. https://taniameacher.com/what-are-somatic-therapy-exercises-for-healing-trauma

Willard, C. (2020, June). *Mindfulness for Kids. Mindful.* https://www.mindful.org/mindfulness-for-kids/

Chapter 6

Awareness and Education. Stanford Neurodiversity Project. (n.d.). https://med.stanford.edu/neurodiversity/education.html

Baumer, N., Frueh, J. (2021, November). *What Is Neurodiversity?. Harvard Health Publishing.* https://www.health.harvard.edu/blog/what-is-neurodiversity-202111232645

DCEG. (2022, April). *Neurodiversity - NCI. dceg.cancer.gov.* https://dceg.cancer.gov/about/diversity-inclusion/inclusivity-minute/2022/neurodiversity

Leadibitter, K., Buckle, K. L., Ellis, C., & Dekker, M. (2021). *Autistic Self-Advocacy and the Neurodiversity Movement: Implications for Autism Early Intervention Research and Practice . Frontiers in Psychology* , 12. https://doi.org/10.3389/fpsyg.2021.635690

Neurodiversity Hub - Resources for Students, Employers & More. Neurodiversity Hub. (n.d.). https://www.neurodiversityhub.org/

Shmulsky, S. (2022). *Neurodiversity Is Diversity. AAC&U.* https://www.aacu.org/liberaleducation/articles/neurodiversity-is-diversity

Stanford Neurodiversity Project. Stanford Neurodiversity Project. (n.d.). https://med.stanford.edu/neurodiversity.html

What the creative industry needs to know about neurodivergence | D&AD Annual 2023. www.dandad.org. (n.d.). https://www.dandad.org/annual/2023/editorial/voices-what-the-creative-industry-needs-to-know-about-neurodivergence

Chapter 8

Duarte, A., Gomes, D., Ribeiro, N., Semedo, A. (2021, May). *Authentic Leadership and Improved Individual Performance: Affective Commitment and Individual Creativity's Sequential Mediation. Frontiers in Psychology.* None

Face Masks and COVID-19. NIH News in Health. (2021, October). https://newsinhealth.nih.gov/2021/11/face-masks-covid-19

Garcia, E., Keane, M. (2022, April). *How "unmasking" leads to freedom for autistic and other neurodivergent people : Life Kit. NPR.org.* https://www.npr.org/2022/04/14/1092869514/unmasking-autism-more-inclusive-world

Gillis Chapman, S. (2019, July). *How Mindful Communication Makes Us More Compassionate. Mindful.* https://www.mindful.org/stop-go-wait/

Mayo Clinic. (2020, August). *Can Face Masks Protect against the coronavirus?. Mayo Clinic.* https://www.mayoclinic.org/diseases-conditions/coronavirus/in-depth/coronavirus-mask/art-20485449

Navigating Text Conversations with Narcissists: Strategies for Assertive and Empathetic Interactions | Integrative Psych. www.integrative-psych.org. (n.d.). https://www.integrative-psych.org/resources/navigating-text-conversations-with-narcissists-strategies-for-assertive-and-empathetic-interactions

Sartor, C., Sunkel, C. (2021, May). *Perspectives: Involving Persons with Lived Experience of Mental Health Conditions in Service delivery, Development and Leadership. BJPsych Bulletin.* None

Chapter 9

Dowling, D. (2017, March). *Balancing Parenting and Work Stress: A Guide. Harvard Business Review.* https://hbr.org/2017/03/balancing-parenting-and-work-stress-a-guide

Hopler, W. (2022, May). *Thriving Together Series: How Communication Can Strengthen Diversity and Inclusion at Work - Center for the Advancement of Well-Being. Center for the Advancement of Well-Being.* https://wellbeing.gmu.edu/thriving-together-series-how-communication-can-strengthen-diversity-and-inclusion-at-work/

Neurodiversity Community Self-Advocate, Writer, Author, and Public Speaker Archives. Autism Spectrum News. (n.d.). https://autismspectrumnews.org/organization/neurodiversity-community-self-advocate-writer-author-and-public-speaker/

Praslova, L. (2021, December). *Autism Doesn't Hold People Back at Work. Discrimination Does. Harvard Business Review.* https://hbr.org/2021/12/autism-doesnt-hold-people-back-at-work-discrimination-does

*The Path of Self-Awareness in the Workplace: Embracing Your Authentic Self - Galt Foundation. * (2023, November). https://galtfoundation.org/2023/11/08/path-self-awareness-embrace-authentic-self/

U.S. Department of Justice Civil Rights Division. (2022). *Guide to disability rights laws. ADA.gov.* https://www.ada.gov/resources/disability-rights-guide/

U.S. Equal Employment Opportunity Commission. (2013, May). *Persons with Intellectual Disabilities in the Workplace and the ADA | U.S. Equal Employment Opportunity Commission. www.eeoc.gov.* https://www.eeoc.gov/laws/guidance/persons-intellectual-disabilities-workplace-and-ada

Made in United States
Troutdale, OR
08/17/2024

22101480R00113